Nobody Cares,

Work Harder

Emily Rose Hubbard

Dedicated to my "Pawpaw," James (Jim) Hubbard for blessing me with his sense of humor and extraordinary determination, and to my "Grandma Dee" Deanna (Dee) Hubbard for her never-ending kindness and generosity towards my family and me.

Table of Contents

Thank you to everyone who's offered me a helping hand during my whirlwind of dream chasing thus far including my family members, friends, and vendors. You all make my world go 'round and your constant belief in me is what gives me the courage to keep going. From early morning shop renovations to late-night brainstorming sessions, I couldn't begin to imagine where I'd be today without you guys. And to my customers, thank you for your choice to shop local and support small business in general. On behalf of the whole One Rose Décor team, we appreciate not only your purchases but also your decision to just spend time in our little boutique.

I'd be a motivational speaker if I had the nerve to speak in front of large crowds. But unfortunately, I don't think anyone wants to stand in a crowd and listen to me stammer. Not to mention, it's 2020 and large gatherings are no longer a thing. So here we are. In a book. Words on a page. Hi, how ya doin?

"I'd love to do something like this BUT...," says a whole bunch of women who walk through my store. After the "but" usually comes a list of reasons why they don't take the leap and just do it. After owning my own business for 4+ years, I've become all too familiar with what women *want* in life, and the reasons why they *think* it's not possible. I've listened to my fair share of excuses, and it's time we, as women, take a stand. It's time we stop listening to our doubtful self-sabotaging thoughts, and start wiping the dust off our confidence.

Let's be real, maybe owning a storefront isn't your jam. Your goals are totally different than mine, and that's totally okay! Maybe you want to start an online store, partner up with somebody who's already started a business, invent a new product, or write a book. Shoot, maybe your goals aren't career-driven at all. Not all of us want to be self-employed (I don't blame you). Maybe you want to connect with old friends, lose weight, save money, or just make more time for your family. Within all of us, there is *something* that we want. There's something that we feel we can't grasp for one reason or another.

Think about your desires right now. Why don't you currently have it? What's stopping you? I'd be willing to bet there are a couple things standing in your way such as fear of possible failure or lack of funds. The roadblocks can seem endless. I'm here to tell you; to change your outcomes you have to change your *mindset*. And to change your mindset, you have to believe these roadblocks don't exist.

Sure, we all have busy lives. We have kids and families who depend on us. We have a million to-do lists piling up each day, and we all have people that we don't want to disappoint. For a minute, let's just ignore those. Would your life look any differently? What would you change about your accomplishments and goals? Image for a second that you could genuinely do anything that you want in life.

Because you can…

Everything you want is within reach. I was 22- years-old and dead broke when I opened my vintage gift store and by the time I turned 25, I had expanded it twice, added on a small café, and bought a bus to go with it. Built in the 1940s, my building has the charm and character that I have long waited for, and is now full of all sorts of up-cycled treasures. My store is comprised of the main lobby, dining area, 6 motel suites, original living quarters, and we share the remaining units with a few other small businesses. It's a little strip of small businesses all run by individuals with a dream and a passion for what they do. A strip of creative minds who've all worked hard to make… it… work…

There are often nights where you'd find all of the tenants there into the wee hours. As you may know, being self-employed doesn't mean 9-5. On most days it means you stay until the job is done, no matter how late that is.

A typical morning pulling into Grove Rd, is to see everybody putting in WORK. Doing what they have to do to keep their businesses afloat, which is what entrepreneurship is all about - doing what you have to do in order to get the job done. This could mean staying after hours and often into the next morning, doing some of the not-so-fun work, and somehow still getting the job done even when you have little to no help from others.

I fondly remember during the renovation process of my first storefront when none of my toilets were in working condition and I'd be forced to pee outside around the corner of the building in the middle of the night. I mean, at 3:00 if nobody else is around, a girl's gotta do what a girl's gotta do, right? 3:00am is too early to quit and go home just when your dream is within reach. During the early stages of shop renovations, that still goes down in history as one of my most vivid memories. Like I said, it ain't always pretty. It was almost difficult to actually pee because I would always be laughing hysterically and constantly wondering if some creeper might be lurking somewhere nearby. Luckily, we did eventually get the toilets up and running before opening day. You're welcome.

It's moments like these make me think of just how hard small business owners and entrepreneurs work and remind me of my very humble beginnings. Whatever it takes, you get the job done. You accept help when it's offered but it's rare that you ask for it and you stop at *literally* nothing. What can I say, you pee outside if you have to? And you'd never hear me complain about it.

We have become so accustomed to making excuses for ourselves because our aspirations can seem so daunting. Looking at my first storefront, it needed so much work. I needed to buy so much inventory because I had nothing. It can seem so easy and effortless to throw in the towel. I had every excuse in the book to choose a different career path and a perfectly useable education degree from VCU that came with solid job offerings.

We don't go to the gym because we don't have time. We don't start that online boutique because we don't have enough money. We don't chase our dreams fully because we are so petrified of falling on our faces or wasting our precious time.

We get in our own way! The only person in charge of you and your life, is yourself and you. I hope that by the time you put this book down, you are feeling refueled, rejuvenated, and ready to take on the world, whatever that may mean for you. I hope you learn from my mistakes but also take inspiration from the things that I've done right along the way. And most of all, I hope that you find it within your heart to be completely obsessed with your life and the person you *can* become. You have a right to be totally and entirely yourself.

If you're looking to build your own career or simply start a side hustle, we all begin with one thing; our innate passions. Our natural God-given talents and interests. Don't know where to start? Start there. What are you interested in? What sets your soul on fire? You can make a living or at least some side money off of anything as long as you're willing to put the work behind it and find a creative way to get there.

With genuine faith and confidence in ourselves and our abilities, the world arrives at our fingertips asking *what's next*? The difference between you and the person who succeeded prior to you is that when they wanted to stop, they kept going. You have to keep pushing. You will either find an excuse, or you will find a way.

"With genuine faith and confidence in ourselves and our abilities, the world arrives at our fingertips asking what's next?"

Sorry to break it to you, I don't have the answers for you in these next 150 pages, but you do. I've narrowed this book down to my 14 favorite and most useful traits that I believe are required to finally see your worth and confidently chase your dreams.

No matter what field you work in or what your specific life goals are, use these following 14 traits to unlock your full potential, light a fire under you, and become the confident woman that you were meant to be in order to obtain those dreams. As you read through each trait, I will provide examples from my own crazy life, situations I've learned from, and of course the relevance of each one. I will dive into the importance of following your heart and unapologetically discovering your purpose.

They say that excuses can last a lifetime and opportunities are temporary. I call bullshit. We have the power to make our own opportunities. If we sit around waiting for opportunities to fall into our lap, we'd never accomplish anything. Don't see a door to open? Make one yourself.

We have made great strides as women. I mean, we are killing it. Why stop now? We *literally* can do anything that we want. You are more powerful than your excuse and you're worth more than what you've grown accustomed to.

humble beginnings

Before we get into the good stuff, let me introduce myself. I came into this world on March 23rd, 1994 at 5:45pm. I had bleach blonde hair, bright green eyes, and abnormally large ears. Not sure why God felt it necessary to bless me with green eyes but leave me with huge ears. Nevertheless, it's just an insecurity of mine that I deal with day-to-day and tend to hate wearing my hair in any kind of updo that exposes my ears. My biggest fears in life are throwing up and growing old. That's normal, right? My favorite food is pasta from Crab Louie's, which is a relatively new discovery. Before that, it was a Philly cheesesteak from the food court in the mall. Favorite color; turquoise in a very light shade (My love for muted, neutral colors can't get down with the bright teals). Favorite thing to do outside of work: work some more. My taste in music will always remain a mystery to me… I enjoy anything from classic bluegrass to eardrum-rupturing EDM. I'm extremely OCD and very creative at the same time, which isn't always the best combo because it's impossible to keep my workshop clean even though I crave tidiness. My ultimate favorite feeling is being barefoot outside in the grass, especially if it's raining. Easiest way to make me cry is show me pictures of puppies or videos of random people getting married. I enjoy long, romantic walks through thrift stores and not-so-fancy dinners at Applebee's. My ideal Friday night is watching crime documentaries from the floor of my living room with a paint brush in one hand and a chicken wing in the other.

I'm just a 20-something-year-old store owner with the desire to create, experiment, and inspire along the way. I will never be the girl who settles for a 9-5 and a steady paycheck just to obtain stability. Instead, you can find me either digging through junk at a thrift store or in a Dunkin' Donuts drive-thru, most always sporting a messy bun and likely without a bra, in fearless pursuit of my dreams.

I was 19-years-old when I started painting furniture and finally finding a way to make a profit off my talents. If you're a maker, you know the amount of time and money you put into things doesn't always leave much room for profitability. It's taken me years to find the sweet spot for price points and taken me even longer to learn how to say no to buying things that are too expensive. My good friend Mary and I shared a sketchy studio apartment on the corner of Grove and Belvedere. Back then, you could say we had a lot of free time on our hands, so we regularly scoured the Goodwill stores in the area for forgotten treasures and vintage gems. On this particular day, we had discovered a small wooden coffee table. Not anything special, and certainly not an antique by any means, but it was cheap and didn't need a whole lot of work so naturally we went ahead and purchased it along with a couple other little odds and ends. We waited patiently in the front seats of her dad's rusty 1960s Chevy for the workers to load up our "ten-dollar-treasure" into the bed of the truck.

All of a sudden, I reached my left arm over to the driver's seat and slapped Mary in the chest. This was the kind of gut reaction type of slap that is performed reflexively and only in case of emergency. Kind of like when you're riding in the passenger seat of your grandma's car and she slams on the brakes a little too hard and instinctively reaches over to hold you back from flying through the windshield. This particular emergency happened to be... DUN DUN DUN... an ex-boyfriend sighting! But not just any ex-boyfriend, oh no. This was the first guy you'd ever dated who was older than you, the first guy who got you in some real-life trouble, the first boyfriend to make your parents realize your taste in men is not so great. Yup, that was the guy loading up our truck.

I sluggishly slumped down as far as I could go into the passenger seat pretending to be busy texting on my phone and waited for this awkward encounter to be over. Unfortunately, my camouflage skills were not so smooth. He quickly recognized me and sparked a conversation while the other men finished loading up the truck. I pretended to be interested, giving a fake laugh paired with a fake smile every now and then. I made small talk without giving up too many details of my current life, and then politely said goodbye and we hastily drove off.

Little did I know that this awkward encounter would be the jumpstart to my career.

We pulled into the parking lot at our apartment, hopped out of the truck, and realized that this man had loaded up not one item, not two items, but a whole armful of furniture pieces into our truck.

Was this a mistake because he wasn't the sharpest tool in the shed? Possibly. Was this a lousy attempt to make me need to contact him or have to make a second trip back to the store? Very likely. Either way, Mary and I had a large apartment that was basically empty at the time. We needed to fill it with furniture and her dad was already on his way to pick the truck back up and take it home. Call us selfish, but we kept all the furniture for ourselves.

I called these pieces our ugly ducklings. I mean, these things were hideous. Drawers didn't slide smoothly, old finishes chipping off, hinges not installed properly. We had every problem from the furniture up-cycling handbook right in front of us and no experience to properly fix it all.

I painted my very first dresser, coffee table, and end table. Looking back now, that was the ugliest, brightest shade of red that I could have possibly picked out. Not to mention, the smelliest. For a reason unknown to me, I used exterior paint on a piece of furniture that would literally never sit outside a day in its life. Clearly, the stress of school was getting to me because that just flat out didn't make sense because there's numerous lines of paint designed specifically for furniture. If you're at all familiar with exterior paint, you know it reeks to high heaven. And yes, every resident complained about the stench for about a week. Whoops! They weren't very fond of me by the time I moved out, but can you blame them?

After what felt like an eternity of experimenting with many different types of paint, countless styles of furniture, and selling a boatload of items out of my small, run-down apartment downtown, I finally opened my own storefront. A whopping 200 square feet. If you're not well-versed in the terms of square footage, this was about the length of one adult cartwheel. We aren't talkin' small business here, we are talking TINY business.

Although I've only been a store owner for about 4 years, after outgrowing multiple locations and tackling many obstacles, I've learned an abundance of life lessons and have plenty of insight bursting at the seams that I just have to share with you.

Within these 14 traits, I will provide you with my life experiences, examples, insight, and much more so that you can take this information and use it to guide you through this crazy thing we call self-employment. Enjoy the journey!

commitment

Committing yourself to a constant forward motion

Let's kick this off with one of my favorite traits, commitment. This is a topic that I personally enjoy talking about because it can really apply to anyone and to just about any life, job, or side hustle. What are you doing if you're not constantly committed toward a forward motion? Committed to your goals? You know it's time for change when you find yourself getting comfortable. There's not a more perfect place to insert a quote from my man Trevor Hall: "If you're feeling like you've stopped learning, if the wood in your fire ain't burning, you better spark a match, start turning your wheel. You better turn it so it's right. Start living."

I'll be honest, I struggled long and hard with what to title this chapter. So many traits have come to mind that I find so important, but I kept circling back around to this one, this one word that holds so much value. Beyond all other traits discussed in this book, commitment is at the core of all of them. Sure, you can have goals, desires and dreams, but they're meaningless without being fully committed to them.

By being committed, you're making a promise to yourself to not only know what you want, but also to have the courage to get yourself there no matter what happens along the way. And no matter how impossible it might seem at first.

In the world of small business, let's face it, there's a lot of us chasing similar goals. It's hard enough to compete with others but sometimes it's even harder to compete with ourselves. Not only are you responsible for your own destiny, but you're also your own worst critic. I actively try to shift my focus away from trying to be better than those around me and commit to just being better than last week's version of myself.

Around age 14, I was a national figure skating finalist, which is where my desire to "be better" began. I started skating when I was just about 5-years-old. At the time, my little bird legs couldn't even support the weight of my clunky roller skates. Every time I picked one of my feet up off the ground, it looked like my poor little leg was trying to lift a 100 lb. boulder on wheels. After years of growing into my skates, I finally began entering competitions.

Slowly, I started coming in higher and higher in the rankings. I went from doing local competitions to competing at the U.S.A. National Figure Skating

Competition where I was placing at or near the top most every time. But let's not forget the real victory here – my skates finally looked proportional to my body by this time!

I was so incredibly focused on beating the other girls that I would forget to look at my own score sheet. Instead of walking over to the DJ booth and checking my own numbers, I would wait for the announcer to come over the intercom and announce our rankings. I was committed to being better than my competition rather than being committed to my *own* goals.

Not many people my age were competitive roller skaters at that time. I mean, it's not your typical sport, so things started to get pretty repetitive the older I got. I was consistently skating against the same group of 12 or so girls at every competition. I began to memorize their names, their hairstyles, their outfits, and could always predict the order that we would all place in at the end of the day. There was me and 3 other girls who would take turns winning the gold. It was always a toss-up between the three of us there for a couple of years, and every time I was guilty of allowing my jealousy to get the better of me when I would come in second or third behind them. It became more of a mission for me to take the other girls down than it was to actually improve my own scores. I would have been perfectly happy with a gold medal each time, even if my scores were less than they were during the previous competition. It was so easy for me to forget that I was really only competing against myself.

Life isn't a race against others, and neither is your job. It's not about how many stores you can open in the span of one short year. It's not about how many vendors you can jam pack into your boutique. And it's not about how many times you come in top 3 at a skate competition. If your small business or side hustle doesn't set a fire inside your soul and it's not the motivation behind your drive, then you're in it for the wrong reasons. And let me tell you, having a "real job" could be a whole lot easier than employing yourself!

We have to start learning to focus more on ourselves and less on others around us. Commit yourself to becoming a better version of *you*. Getting comfortable: No good. You can feel it when its coming, too. It hits you like the plague. It's so easy to fall into a rut, a pattern, and sticking with the same easily reachable goals for far too long. The whole point of setting a goal is to set it slightly above what you think to be achievable. That way when you start hitting that goal every month, week, day, then it's time to raise the bar for yourself. When things start to feel easy, move! Light a fire under your butt and go!

Getting too comfortable is how you end up tripping over yourself. You get so used to coming into work and doing what's easy. Remember, YOU are the boss here. Things don't move forward unless you make them move forward. Your business and your self-confidence will stay in one place forever if you allow it.

It's also important to remember that staying committed isn't always going to be going forward continuously. Sometimes you will have to go backwards for a short period in order to move forward in the long run. Think of it as a general picture rather than just right here and right now. If you look at the progression of small businesses on a graph, the line should resemble a heartbeat. Up, down, up, down. Don't get discouraged. You are powerful, you are unique, your ideas are gold, and you're in control of your own life and success.

Loving yourself unapologetically

In case you haven't heard, loving yourself is totally IN right now. It's a topic that we all like to dance around but often choose to avoid facing head-on; however, in the world of building my own brand, creating a company, or managing a side gig, loving and valuing myself as a person has to come first.

Without self-respect as a priority, everything else will inevitably fall short.

I would be lying if I said those early years of figure skating didn't contribute, in some way, to my low self-esteem. Don't get me wrong, I absolutely loved skating and I talk all the time about how I wish I was still competing, but this was the first time I was exposed to any kind of competition. It was the first time that I was being judged...literally. But let me tell you something about figure skating. You don't *just* get judged on the way you skate. Crazy concept, right? You practice for months and months to end up getting points taken off for wearing the wrong bra (or lack thereof), having a few hairs out of place, or having your skates tied incorrectly. I was a master of religiously doing these things wrong. Every. Single. Time. I taught myself how to tie my own shoes when I was a little girl and I always insisted on pinning up my own hair. Needless to say, I was always looking like a hot mess. And wear a bra under my already

tight and uncomfortable outfit? Forget about it.
Honestly, it's a mystery that I ever placed at all.

For as long as history has been recorded,
women have been conditioned to embody low self-
esteem. Society has mastered all the tricks to channel
the deepest depths of your inner self-doubt, whether it
be physical or mental. As women, it seems like
society is always trying to shape us into this perfect
cookie-cutter mold. We are supposed to wear a size 2,
have tan skin year-round (which doesn't even make
sense), cater to the endless needs of others, and only
speak when spoken to.

As I'm sure we all know, people have a
tendency to be unnecessarily critical of one another.
Take it from me, the overly skinny, bucktooth girl that
had to wear her headgear out in public. Yes, I said
headgear. Sure, we all had things that we've been
bullied for over the years, but let's just be honest, it
doesn't get more humiliating than having a metal
brace protruding from your face and extending all the
way around the back of my head. Cute, I know.

Just when I thought it couldn't get any worse, plot twist - I discovered that it was magnetic! Yup, there was 12-year-old me, sitting in my parent's living room sticking refrigerator magnets to my face. Again, cute.

My orthodontist informed me that I was required to wear this monstrosity for a certain number of hours per day. Being that it was impossible to sleep with, I was left with no other choice but to wear it out into...dare I say it, public during the day! I've certainly never been one to turn down a challenge. If I was supposed to wear it for 5 hours a day, I'd easily wear it for 6 or 7, no questions asked, which meant if I had to run errands with my mom, I was in headgear. If I had to stay after school one day, I was in headgear. If I had to go to family dinner, I was in headgear. Basically, if I wasn't asleep or showering, I was sporting this thing around my face. And let me tell ya, it wasn't easily ignored. I would often get asked what was wrong with me or why I was wearing it, which I'm sure is no shock to those of you reading this. Leaving the house, I knew what was in store for me.

Now, I could sit here, lie to you, and say that I was the "popular" kid. The one who always had the boys chasing after her, the one who got straight A's and still somehow had time for a thriving social life. My friends and I were so totally immersed in our own world that we didn't have a clue on how to be "popular."

For example, in middle school (private school), I was apparently the only person who ever folded their clothes after switching into gym attire. *I'm sorry that I didn't want to put wrinkly clothes back on after gym class for the rest of the day.* The other girls would constantly laugh, point, and ask me why I wanted to fold my clothes. I did it anyway, every day until gym class was no longer a requirement, *thank goodness*. I had boys ask me out on dates as a joke. Of course, when I would say yes, I would hear a swarm of their best buds laughing in the background. I've been told that I'm ugly, (and when I say "told," I actually mean that it was belted at full volume across the school track for the entire class to hear). I've been told I have "grandma legs" because of cellulite, which I now dramatically and jokingly refer to as my "craters." I've been told that I look anorexic, but also told that I will "never be skinny enough." I've been labeled as a prude but then also labeled as a slut. I've been called a screwup, sucker, a stupid, scuzzlebutt, and pretty much everything else under the sun, as I'm sure we all have.

The funny thing is, my weight has always been considered by a doctor to be "average" for my height. I've learned over the years that when there's nothing for people to ridicule you for, they will make things up. You can't please everyone, so you might as well please yourself. After all, being yourself is the easiest and most effortless thing to do.

Surround yourself with people who make you feel good about yourself. If you date somebody who tells you that "you'll never be skinny enough," do yourself a favor and kick that person to the curb in your red high heels.

Just remember, the boys who made fun of you in middle school will also be the boys who apologize profusely to you later on and try to buy you drinks at the bar. And I got to tell ya, it feels damn good to turn that drink down. *Or to throw it on them, but you didn't hear that piece of advice from me.*

Having said all of that, if you're thinking about starting your very own side hustle, it can be so easy to undervalue yourself. You've most likely been conditioned all your life to assume that people aren't always thinking the greatest thoughts about you. And sometimes that's true. *Will people like my product? Will people want to buy from me?* But most importantly*, will people take me seriously?* You assume that since you haven't had much experience, you should be charging less than you do for your goods or services. You assume that because of other previous life experiences, you might get turned down and ultimately fail.

The first signs that I ever sold, I only charged as much as I paid for materials. So essentially, I made a whopping zero dollars. Back in the good ol' days of breaking even, I didn't even care about showing a profit. I yearned to get my products out there at that time, and I was excited that people actually wanted to spend their money on something that I made with my own two hands. But going forward, I knew I had to make myself a pricing guide if I wanted to really grow. I didn't have the time or money to be selling myself short. You are better than that. You deserve better. And let's be honest, if you're planning to make a living at this, you can't afford to sell yourself for anything less. I've always been told, "know your worth, and then add tax."

The key is to rewire the way our brains are programmed to think. There are so many things in this world that are, for the most part, out of our control—the society we live in, what we see on the news, social media posts, and the actions of our peers. We have to remember that the only thing we are personally in control of is the way we react and how we allow ourselves to be affected. These are conscious CHOICES. While reading this, you may think you don't always have control of your thoughts, or at least your immediate ones; however, our brain is a muscle just like any other in our body. We have to exercise it for it to function to the best of its ability. If you believe yourself to be in control of your thoughts, you will be. You'll get better at it with time. If you start to think more highly of yourself and your work, you will start to produce better work and ultimately charge more for it. You'll speak more confidently about yourself without even realizing it.

Staying physically healthy is a big part of this as well. Your brain and mind work best simultaneously. Finding a good mental and physical balance is crucial to establishing self-love. Make time to go to the gym or do activities outdoors. Go for a run or bike around your neighborhood, literally anything to get that blood flowing along with those creative juices. Other than working out, a great way to maintain your physical health is to catch some Zzz's. If we're being real with one another here, we all love sleep. It's free, it's easy, and honestly, my favorite place on earth is inside my comforter cloud.

With a regular gym schedule, a cup of coffee, a good motivational playlist, and a killer outfit, you've got yourself a recipe for success, my friend. Don't forget, you're never fully dressed until you *own* it! *hair flips* Confidence is the hottest outfit, so rock it with style. With a sharp and focused mind, you'll be putting out your very best work and who wouldn't love themselves for that?

You don't need talent as long as

you're curious enough

Ahhh, curiosity. Quite possibly the most overlooked and undervalued of all the traits we'll be discussing in this book. Point in case, this is actually the chapter of my book that I wrote *last*. If we're being honest, I totally forgot about it until the middle of the night one night. That's when all of my best ideas start flowing. Night owl at heart over here.

Curiosity is something that tends to be somewhat subconscious for most of us. We don't normally sit around thinking about what sparks our interest unless somebody asks. Of course, we are all curious about things; however, it's not uncommon for us to ignore them sometimes. We are so easily focused on what our superiors tell us to be focused on. When we're younger, it's our teachers, principals, and parents. In our older years, it's our professors, advisors, and bosses. There is little time left for the things we yearn to know more about whom others may deem irrelevant or unimportant. Have you ever heard the phrase "play is children's work"? This indicates that play is actually productive. Why? Because playing gives children the opportunity to explore what they naturally are curious about and drawn to. Chances are your teachers back in high school didn't give you much free time to explore topics that you wanted to learn more about. Class after class of material that made you want to just take a nap on your desk, which I did my fair share of.

I've spent many hours in English courses during my youth and I can remember one… yes, only one… time when I was allowed to write about something that I had the freedom to choose myself. It took me up until my junior year in college to get to this point, which isn't surprising. Curriculum nowadays is so jam-packed with other material that if a teacher even takes one day off, it throws off her lesson plan for the rest of the semester. After being alive for 26 years and being in school for a majority of that time, a teacher was finally giving me some freedom. I honestly wasn't even sure what to do with it at first. This was a Women's Sexuality class, a class that I had chosen to take as an elective because frankly, who doesn't want to sit around talking about boobs and equal rights all day? Easy A, right? The task at hand was to write about basically anything that involved feminism in some sort of way. Way to go professor... keeping us all "on topic" but also giving us an appropriate amount of freedom. Love it.

My options for topics were essentially endless. I immediately chose to examine my all-time favorite movie, *Alice In Wonderland*. Now, obviously this movie has been remade quite a number of times, and normally in my opinion "the older the better," but I can't say no to Johnny Depp so I went with the most modern remake. It ended up working in my favor because turns out the references to feminism in this 21st century version of the movie was off the charts and I had plenty of content to write about in my essay.

The setting of the movie may have been 1865, but Alice Pleasance Liddell didn't take no crap from no man! I flew through the assignment with ease. In honor of finally getting an A on a college assignment, I displayed it nicely on the front of my refrigerator at home. BAM!

What does *Alice in Wonderland* have to do with painting furniture and owning my own store you might ask? Well, nothing really. My point is, when I found myself immersed in something that I was totally curious about, it was a slam dunk paper. Like I said, easy A. I found this assignment to not only be the most fascinating, quickest paper I'd ever written, but also the most delightful. Finally, a piece of homework that I actually… dare I say it, enjoyed?!

As an elementary education major, I do acknowledge the importance of structured activities and sticking to a curriculum, but I can't ever seem to ignore how good it always made me feel to have a little bit of freedom when it came to learning. Curiosity is the driving force behind passion and motivation. I'm a huge supporter of encouraging curiosity within schools, workplaces, and life in general. The mind of a curious person is an active mind, always thinking and eager to learn. The more curious you are about something, the more energy and dedication you'll give towards knowing and accomplishing more.

I am totally and undoubtedly motivated 100% by curiosity. As Alice would say, "curiouser and curiouser." When I want to know more about something, I get completely invested in it. I'd be willing to guarantee none of my friends saw me for about two weeks when I was in the midst of writing that *Alice In Wonderland* paper. At this point in my life my friends are well aware that if I go MIA for a little while, I'm most likely working on some crazy project or discovered a new hobby. If I need to know how to assemble a part on my old camper, you can find me three hours later sucked into the depths of YouTube watching tutorials and attempting to teach myself the ropes.

The most interesting parts of my job are the ones that I find myself most curious about. Dealing with old buildings, old vehicles, and old furniture, I find a lot of weird junk, let's just say that. The ultimate gold mine is when I pull the drawer out from an old chest and find handwritten notes or recipes within. Sometimes they're nicely placed on the bottom of the drawer, facing up as if they were waiting to be found and read. Other times, you'll find them balled up and shoved towards the back of the chest, hidden in a corner that probably would never have been unearthed if it weren't for somebody trying to restore the piece of furniture. I'll find the occasional love letters, notes to grandkids about the hand-me-down piece of furniture, reminders, notes to friends, grocery lists, etc. These long-forgotten items always make me curious. *Why did somebody leave this behind? Isn't somebody going to eventually need this recipe from 1930? Who is Tommy and why was he sending a post card to his parents from a motel?*

When you realize the age behind a piece, it makes you step back and think of all the things it has been through, how many owners it has had, and where it sat for so many years. I can't help but wonder what the walls would say if they could talk. These are the things that make it that much more special when bringing a piece of furniture back to life. It's a special and delicate job to be able to do justice to an old piece.

Although, sometimes you may not want to know what lies within its history. I may be a curious person, but I'm not curious about everything! Nobody needs to know what's on those homemade VHS porn tapes, Sally! Yes, this was a real discovery of mine, and no I didn't watch them!

intuition

Navigating life's tough choices
by following your innate passions

Piggybacking off of curiosity, I'd like to talk about intuition. During our younger years, we are kind of just going through the motions. Like I've said, we go to school, and we do all of these things that we're told to do, and we do it without asking questions. We turn 18 and we're supposed to immediately know what we want to do with our lives. When do we have time to really figure ourselves out?

How do we know at 18-years-old what we're supposed to be doing for the rest of our lives?

I'll tell you, at 18-years-old, I was a full-time student studying education (had already switched my major once and was considering switching it again), mindlessly chasing boys, trying to get my personal training certification on the side, and was serving pizza at Skate-A-Way while also working at Cici's. At this point, I had never even considered painting a piece of furniture. Honestly, I didn't even know that was a "thing."

Fast forward 6 years, I'm doing a whole lot of NOTHING with my education degree, I have my own furniture store, and haven't stepped foot in a roller skate since the day I quit my job there. Don't get me wrong, I still have a passion for skating, but no desire to serve pizza.

Point being, you don't have to know what you want to do with your life right away. It's not catastrophic if you haven't decided on a major the day after your high school graduation. Ladies, it's okay! I can tell you though, that I'm sure you've known all along what you want to do. Sometimes it just takes a while for that desire to surface and become apparent. It takes a little time and a lot of mistakes to find that passion sometimes.

Your gut will always tell you what's right. Think about what you love, think about what your passions are, think about the things in life that genuinely make you feel pure happiness. That, my dear, is what you should be following. For some, it's obvious. For others, not so much. But deep down, we are all made for *something*. It's built into the fibers of our being. It's your job to pursue it and not ignore those desires, even if it seems impossible. Obviously, this isn't just for those of you who want to open a small business, but whatever it is that you're passionate about – Go. For. It. Simply put, "follow your gut."

I was just a young girl without a care in the world when I would hear this all the time. *Mom, what do you mean "listen to my gut"?* Realistically, If I'm actually listening to my gut, chances are it's telling me to down a cheeseburger and a large fry with extra ranch dipping sauce. I never quite knew what this phrase really meant until I entered my adult life. Growing up, I was so naïve, as most of us were in our younger years. I flew through life with ease during those years, always doing as I was told until I got to the point where nobody was telling me what to do anymore. All of a sudden, I was feeling so much pressure to do the right things on my own, and along with that came tremendous stress.

When I was younger, my friends would always ask me why I enjoyed doing the things that I enjoyed doing. Being so young, I didn't always have calculated answers. I would kind of just shrug innocently. I wanted to make scrapbooks, I wanted to paint things, I wanted to redecorate my room. My hobbies always came naturally to me and I didn't know why I was being expected to explain it so often. I didn't know that girls wanted to do other things. Don't get me wrong, I definitely had my Bratz dolls and Polly Pocket phases, but overall my creative mind took over whatever activity we were doing. Even when I played with my Barbie dolls, I wanted to build houses for them rather than just dress them up. I would gather up old shoe boxes and tape them together. Some had just one floor and others were full blown multi-floor shoebox mansions. And let me tell you, these weren't your typical makeshift doll houses. These homes had painted walls, makeshift furniture, carpet on the floors, and wallpaper lining each room. This was like real life *Fixer Upper*: Barbie Dreamhouse Edition. Each was so intricate, down to even the magnets that I created to stick on the little 4-inch-tall refrigerator made out of old cereal boxes or whatever scrap paper I could find laying around. The funny part is, once I would complete my Barbie house reno, I wouldn't even want to actually play with the dolls. I would just pack it up and go search my grandparent's attic for some more shoeboxes and start all over. Barbie real estate—it was serious business!

In every phase of life, my natural hobbies and talents were extremely apparent. I was very obviously drawn to the more creative sides of things, so when it came time to decide on which high school to attend, obviously my first choice was a school with an art program. My mom of course advised me to apply to a few more "backup choices" as well, which I did.

Shockingly, I was turned down by the one art program that I applied to. I was left with no choice but to spend my high school career in Matoaca's technology program. Me? Technology? Yeah, I had no clue what I was doing but what other option did I have? During my interview, the only thing I had to offer on my resume was that I was "super awesome" at editing my HTML code on my Myspace page. Somehow, advanced Myspace coding was enough to get me into their specialty program but a full-blown art portfolio that I had worked on for years was not up to par. Still makes no sense to me.

After completing all of my required computer courses, I immediately signed myself for AP art, AP photography, and any other creative course that was offered. No matter how many schools told me that I wasn't good enough, it was impossible for me to stray from my intuition. My gut told me to follow my passion for art no matter what circumstances I was presented with.

Soon into my early twenties, I began finding myself in a position where I was torn between multiple things. Growing up, I had always heard that adult life comes with a lot of hard choices but never really internalized what that actually meant until now. I was finally experiencing this for the first time at the start of freshmen year at Radford (again, not my first choice of schools). Between a very messy personal life, full time class schedule, discovering my passion for furniture painting, and juggling multiple part-time jobs, I had an abundance of decisions to make and they weren't coming easily anymore.

I spent one semester at Radford University where I studied art education. When first entering college, I anticipated being surrounded by fellow art majors who were passionate about their studies. I mean, this is college now, doesn't everybody take their classes seriously? Wrong. My first night there, the streets were flooded with drunken idiots. And by "flooded," I mean you literally couldn't even navigate through the mass of people in the streets. Of course, the first week was always the craziest, but to be honest it didn't die down a whole lot throughout the course of the semester.

Don't get me wrong, I've had my fair share of party days. Ask my best friend Mandy about the high school house parties we went to. These weren't your typical house parties where you go and get tipsy with your girlfriends and then still make it home before curfew. These were the type of parties where you would be found either dancing on tabletops or on the verge of dying in a field from alcohol poisoning. If you're from my hometown, you know that Matoaca High School is essentially in the middle of nowhere. So, when a kid was throwing a party, it most likely was literally going to take place in an old abandoned building or a horse pasture where there were no cops. Safe to say those days are long gone and we are thankful to have made it out alive!

But as much as I admired the Radford campus itself and the professors that I had, I quickly realized that I was swimming in a sea of frat house douche bags and self-tanned Barbie dolls. I related to these people in no way, shape, or form. And believe me, I tried. Once again, I found myself trying to be something that I wasn't. I was straying further and further away from the things that I had naturally been drawn to my entire life. I went to more than my fair share of frat parties. Not because I wanted to, but because my guy friends would beg me to go and I was terrible at saying no. If you aren't too familiar with college life, let me clue you in. A guy isn't allowed entrance to a party unless he has at least one girl with him. Literally, there is a girl to guy ratio required for entry. Didn't have enough girls with you? Sorry bro, can't come in. I would be pried away from my drawing table to be used as an entry ticket most every weekend. I made the most of it. I did have fun. But was I focused on art at all? No. Was I taking my classes seriously? No. Was I feeling a career coming on anytime soon? Big negative.

After a few weeks of talking it out with my roommate, lots of pros and cons lists, and a little bit of intuition, I decided to put in my application to transfer to VCU back in my hometown of Richmond. *Ahhhh, home!* Once accepted, I quickly packed my bags, moved out of my dorm from my good friend Haily, left her a hastily scribbled "I'll miss you and I love you" note on our dry erase board, and left before I even had the chance to say goodbye in person. I moved in with my childhood friend Mary and finished my college career 5 years later, graduating with a bachelor's degree in elementary education.

How ironic that I felt more at home at VCU studying education than I ever did at Radford studying art. I guess it just goes to show that you really "are who you hang out with." If you've ever been to the city of Richmond, VA, I'm sure you're familiar with its well-known artsy vibes and creative energies. Even though I was no longer majoring in art, I felt right at home. Tattoo-covered, pink-hair-rockin', highwater-wearing kids. These were my people. I felt comfortable. In Richmond, I was able to wear what I wanted, I could draw and doodle during class and not be stared at, I could paint in between classes and not have people wondering if I had a couple screws loose. I could be myself and people wouldn't even look twice. I was totally in my element.

My mom used to tell me all the time, "you become who you surround yourself with." Being younger and a whole lot more naïve than I am now, I never quite understood or agreed with this. But once at VCU, I could finally see where she was coming from. Richmond and VCU completely embrace art. Everybody feeds off each other's creative juices and it's downright awesome. There were people of every race and color, every body type, every style of clothing, and every tattoo imaginable (you'd surely find it on somebody's skin on the VCU campus). If you could think of a random idea for a school club, it probably already existed. It wasn't unusual to walk past Monroe Park and see a large mass of people dressed like Star Wars characters and fighting with light sabers. Not that I can specifically relate to that on *any* level, but the point is there was something for everybody. By following the things that naturally set your soul on fire and surrounding yourself with people of similar interests, there is no other option than to thrive.

A year or so into my VCU studies, I quit my job at Cici's Pizza. This was my very first job straight out of high school. I had just gotten my certification for personal training and always had a passion for working out and helping others live a healthy lifestyle. I had applied for a job at Victory Lady Fitness, an all-women gym right near my apartment that I was living in at the time. Right around that same time, I had also just put in my application to become a part time teacher at a nearby preschool. I got the job at Victory Lady immediately after I applied. I was thrilled, so of course I accepted it right away. I began working there and loved it, but one short week into my gym job, I got a call back from the preschool. They offered me the job that I had applied for. Once again, I found myself torn between two different things that I loved so much. On one hand, I had landed this personal training job that I had worked so hard to get certified for, but on the other hand I had been presented with this great opportunity to really build my teaching resume. I hadn't even finished my official employee training at the gym yet, so obviously I was terrified to tell them that I might be quitting so soon. I distinctly remember posting a Facebook status that night, "what do you do when your gut doesn't tell you which choice to make?" This was one of the first serious adult choices that I had been faced with and truly didn't know how to follow my instincts. Although it seems so insignificant now, at that time I was just learning what my true passions were and trying to figure out what was really important in my life. I was so conflicted.

Both jobs were amazing, and I hadn't yet mastered the art of making difficult decisions, so I ended up doing what was best for my resume. I accepted the preschool position and then had to deal with the consequences that came from that… telling Victory Lady that I was quitting after only one week. I was still on their schedule for the following week, so I had to suck up my pride and work all those shifts instead of just not showing back up. *And yes, I really did contemplate just being a no-show.* I was absolutely terrified of breaking the bad news to them. They had already been paying me for my training hours and now I was useless to them. By taking that position, I had cost other applicants the opportunity. I knew there were multiple people who wouldn't be happy with me, and that's always hard for me to handle even if I know that I'm doing what's best for me. Anybody else have a terrible fear of letting people down? This was one of the big moments in my life that made me realize you have to live rather selfishly. I know that I'm put here on this Earth to follow my passions and become who I'm supposed to become. And that might upset a few people along the way.

I sat in my bed and dialed the phone number but didn't press "call" until about 5 minutes later. I just kept thinking about how weird it was going to be to let them know I accepted another job, but then still have to work my scheduled shifts for the next week. AWKWARD.

Luckily, I ended up surviving those last couple of shifts, started my job at the preschool, and worked there for basically the rest of my college career.

When becoming your own boss and creating something so special, you have to learn how to listen to your gut feelings, your intuition. It will always lead you towards what your heart yearns for, but it's not always easy to carry out. It's not always an obvious choice. Sometimes it takes an outsider to pull it out of you.

I was just a junior in college and still working at the preschool when I began thinking about opening a storefront. I had already founded my business as an LLC about one year prior and at this time I was only doing online sales and selling furniture out of my parent's garage. Opening a storefront was one my many long-term goals but never saw it as possibly becoming reality in the early stages of my business journey until a good friend of mine started beating some confidence into my brain. I would soon find myself torn *again* between two passions.

Jake and I were total opposites, had virtually nothing in common, and eventually grew apart losing much of our communication. That's life, people come and people go, but I'm a firm believer that we meet the people in our lives for a reason. He wasn't meant to stay but he was meant to be present during that time. During the duration of our friendship, I would always joke with him about how I was going to write a book one day and thank him for his never-ending support and faith in somebody that he honestly didn't know very well. So here we are four years later.

"You can do anything you want in life." You hear it all the time. When you're little, your teachers and parents tell you that you can grow up and be President of the United States if you want to. But let's be honest, how many of us actually believe that to be true about ourselves? It's a saying that is often overstated and easily brushed off. Growing up, we hear it so much that we almost become numb to it and it becomes meaningless unless people really make an effort to actively push you or reinforce it. Too many of us set easily achievable standards and goals for ourselves because we don't have enough faith in our capabilities or reason to believe that we can ever become something much more. Or maybe you've established high standards for yourself and just simply don't know where to start in order to pursue them. You want to get there but are unsure of how.

As we progress in life, we hear these encouragements less and less. We are conditioned to believe in our dreams… but only up until a certain point. Right up until we actually start having faith in our goals and then we hear that we need to slow our roll and be more "realistic."

It's hard enough to follow your dreams when you have people backing you, but it's a whole new ballgame of dream chasing when your desires fall outside of the "norm" and even your closest friends and family members are skeptical of your capabilities.

Whether it was roaming the streets of Richmond, climbing onto trains, or exploring abandoned buildings, Jake and I were dreamers; always brainstorming about off-the-wall ideas and totally living in la-la land. He had an undeniable faith in me, and at that time, I had never experienced anyone truly believing in these crazy dreams of mine. He saw it before I ever could imagine that it was possible, and he was the first person to really make me seriously start wondering what I was capable of in life and convinced me to take action.

I had been working at the local preschool for a couple of years by this time and I was so in love with that job, the kids, the parents, and the coworkers that came with it. Even when I was cleaning up poop or throw-up. Out of all the part-time jobs that I've had over the course of my high school and college career, the preschool gig was by far the most enjoyable. Those kids were the best part of my day. My goal of owning a store was becoming more and more plausible and I was beginning to see it happening more clearly by the day. It took me weeks to muster up the courage to quit and move on with my dreams. I sat in Jake's desk chair in his tiny city apartment, staring a hole into his computer screen. I had my email pulled up; I even had the preschool director's name entered into the recipient section. The cursor on the screen blinked at me over and over just waiting for me to type something. I would type, erase, stare at Jake, type some more, erase some more, and then hopelessly look at Jake again. He sat patiently next to me, facing me, chin in his palms. He laughed at me for being so hesitant.

After what seemed like a lifetime, I had finally drafted the perfect two-week notice. Respectful, well-written, and to the point. As I hit send, I'll admit I shed a tear or two. I knew this was the end of an incredible chapter in my life, but I slept peacefully that night knowing the door to my future had finally just been cracked opened.

I savored every minute of my last day on the clock at Westhampton Day School two weeks later. I choked back tears until the second I stepped foot into my car and started to drive off and then all hell broke loose. I sobbed as I scrolled through pictures on my phone of the kids that I knew I had just seen for the last time.

Intuition has always pointed me in the right direction and led me to exactly where I needed to be. I just had to be strong enough to be able to follow it and smart enough to know when it's calling me. You may be different from other people, your friends may have other interests than you, and you might even get picked on for following your passion. That is OKAY! Society likes to tell women what they should and shouldn't be. And I'll be damned if I get married only to be a housewife who's "not allowed to work."

Growing up, my father was always the driving force behind my creative tendencies. In a world of norms and 9-5s, he demonstrated to me that you don't have to fit inside of society's box. He's worked for himself for most of my adult life and been a writer for as long as I can remember. We've had many conversations about the importance of following your dreams no matter what the cost, and I so desperately wish that I could remember all of his exact words to reference them here. All I know is that he made everything sound so simple and easy. Want something? Just go for it. You have a desire to be something? Just be it. Hesitation and second guessing didn't exist for him. I was reminded constantly that worrying about something won't ever change your outcome. The only thing that has an effect on your outcomes are your *actions*. With fearlessness and a quirky sense of humor, he showed this bucktooth freckle faced 5-year-old girl that she could be anything she wanted in life and that taking the world by storm should be effortless. You see, being unapologetically yourself is actually very easy once you learn to tune out the expectation's of the world and simply do what feels right to *you*.

We are all existing quietly under a layer of popular opinions, cultural conditioning, and false conclusions that we've come to accept about ourselves during our youth. Life isn't about finding ourselves. Instead, we must return to former self-the self that we were born with. The one that the universe gifted us. We must revert back to that state of mind where acceptance from others was irrelevant, norms were nonexistent, and pleasing people wasn't so dang important.

The balancing act between wants and needs.
And the importance of both.

If we're being honest here, being your own

boss takes a lot of guts and self-control. It may seem

like a breeze from an outside perspective, but without

being in control of yourself, your choices, and your

actions, your business and you will inevitably

crumble. I once heard something from a leasing agent that I will never forget. He said: "If you don't constantly have two feet in, you're going to fail."

Of all the necessary traits that you will need to succeed in the small business world, self-discipline ranks right up there at the top as far as importance. After all, this business and your life have been built from the ground up by none other than yourself. You are in control here and you can't let yourself forget that. Holding so much weight on your shoulders can sometimes feel overwhelming but nobody can bring you back in touch with reality other than yourself. There are plenty of ways to make sure you stay on top of things.

Keep a planner. My planner is basically where my entire brain is housed. Even if you're not a very organized person by nature, I can't tell you enough… this is absolutely necessary! I'll tell you a little bit about my planner. I didn't get one of those little itty-bitty pocket planners, no, I have your full size – as big as you can go – obnoxious – in your face – "wow she's a nerd" type of planner. It's nothing fancy (it came from Walmart for no more than five dollars), BUT it's big, it's organized, and it has plenty of tools in it to get the job done. It has a monthly section as well as a weekly section. I write my daily to-do list on each day within the weekly section, and I write my larger, more important reminders/tasks on the monthly section so that I can see all of that at-a-glance. Daily tasks might include returning somebody's phone call, put an extra layer of paint on that dresser, or scheduling a post on the Facebook page. The more important tasks would include things such as monthly payments (insurance, rent, retail sales tax, etc.), big store events/sales, and due dates for projects. You may not need to have a month AND weekly section. That may be just too much organization for you if you aren't OCD like me. In that case, you could probably get by with just having one or the other (weekly or monthly).

In fact, you may not like a handwritten method at all. Maybe you enjoy using the calendar on your phone instead, which is totally cool because you can be organized on the go! Or even using the calendar on your laptop. Shoot, hang a big calendar up on the wall of your office or store if you need more of an "in-your-face" type of reminder. Whatever your style of organization is, just find something that works for you and stick with it! *Consistency* is key.

Self-discipline is more than just about getting organized and writing down your tasks. It's also about making sure you carry out those tasks. Nobody is watching over your shoulder making sure that you get things accomplished. Nobody is there to tell you how or when to do things. Just because you've written a task down in your planner doesn't mean that a magical fairy is going to come and do it for you. It's all on you. Like I said earlier, business owners wear multiple hats… one of them being the hat of a manager. You are your own manager. You're the boss of yourself. I feel like I shouldn't even have to say this but if you don't do something, it won't get done. Hello! Obvious, right? It should go without saying, but I am guilty of slacking off on tasks and I sometimes need to be reminded that I am the center hub of this whole operation. Even the smallest daily tasks are just as important as the larger monthly tasks. Those little tasks add up. You let one thing go undone, it soon becomes five things that are left undone. And pretty soon, you find yourself falling way behind on larger deadlines and goals. And that's part of the reason why I feel this chapter is so crucial and mustn't be overlooked. It seems so obvious at first—owning your own business requires self-discipline, *duh Emily*. But I'm telling you, it's easier to fall off track than you would believe. Keep on top of those little daily tasks, and the larger ones will feel a whole lot easier and come considerably more naturally.

Feeling overwhelmed can happen so frequently. sssYou have so many things on your plate that *need* to get done as well as things in your brain that you *want* to get done. I'm assuming that if you own your own business or even just a side hustle, you are creative in some way, shape, or form. It may not be creativity in the same form that I have (as each person is built differently) but creativity, nevertheless. Your brain probably runs at a pace of 200 mph and rarely does it ever turn off or slow its roll. Prime example, I'm writing this page at 3:00am. All you have to do is look at something and BAM, a new idea pops into your head. It can be hard to manage at times and sometimes it's hard to know which ideas to focus your energy on and which ideas to just let go.

One of the hardest aspects of self-discipline is separating your "want-to-do's" from the "need-to do's." Personally, I struggle massively with this. This is one of my self-sabotaging qualities, I'll admit it.

Let me give you a great example. My business is divided into 2 core concepts: custom work and retail. This means that I have my boutique where I sell all of our vintage goods. This is my playground. This is where I get to decorate, stage, display, and move inventory around constantly. And on the other hand, I have my custom orders where people request that I do certain projects for them. The retail part to me comes so naturally. I could spend all day every day setting up new displays in the store, creating new inventory, making new vignettes—the works! Custom orders are just the opposite. What I call a "custom order" is when a client walks in and basically tells me exactly what they want done to their piece of furniture or what exactly they want a sign to say and I just have to say "yes ma'am" and create what they want. I swear I am a slave to custom orders. Custom orders are something that One Rose Décor is known for, so it's not easy for me to get away from them. It's not even that I don't enjoy doing them, it's just that my time is very valuable and sometimes these orders don't contribute much to building my actual brand. And there is often so many orders going on at once, that it's impossible for me to catch up on them. On days when I've had about 3 cups of coffee before noon, I can knock out a couple of custom orders before the day ends. But I often find myself piddling around the store, posting on social media, doing some calligraphy—you know, the fun stuff. And there's nobody there to slap me back into reality except me, myself, and I! I've learned that I have to create a to-do list every morning to help me stay on track.

The thing I hate most about self-discipline is making myself wake up at a decent hour every morning. I don't know who these robot women are who can easily wake up at 6am every morning, but I certainly can't relate. I'm lucky to be out of bed by 9:00 most mornings, and it's a miracle if I have left the house by 9:30. Once I'm up, I'm up, and I have all the motivation in the world but there seems to be no cure for my constant desire to sleep in. I always hear about how people who wake up before 9:00 and get their day going are said to be more successful in life. They're more productive during the day, they're more alert and more motivated. I know you don't want to hear it, but ladies, we have to start getting ourselves out of bed earlier.

Make a morning routine. I know first-hand that my worst days are days when I don't have time for a morning routine. I like to wake up, get coffee, answer emails, do a little advertising, and tidy up my apartment so that I can come home to a clean living space later. Making yourself wake up with enough time to get your day started is crucial to how successful the next few hours are going to be. This is self-discipline at its finest. If I can make myself wake up early, I can do anything. *In case you haven't gathered this so far, maybe I just need to make it a little clearer: waking up early is my biggest struggle!* Sure, if you're lucky enough to have a spouse to get you up and out of bed, that's awesome. But we can't always rely on other people. As a woman in control of her own life and her own success, it's your job to get yourself up and running properly, which brings me to possibly the most important paragraph of this book…

We are all given the same number of hours in a day. Obviously, this statement is not an "Emily original." We have all been told this before, but I want to reiterate it. Think about other women your age. Even think about people who are younger than you. Think about what they've accomplished in just a short amount of time. They were all given the same number of hours per day that you've been given. Yes, you could argue that some people are born into money, which helps them out in one way or another. But not all of them, ladies! There have been plenty of women born into money who decided to waste it. The real key to what you do with your 24 hours lies behind your motivation, and your drive to get sh!t done! We are only given a short time on this planet, and in the grand scheme of things, this is a blink of an eye. We have to utilize our time wisely. Every hour of your day, every day, is critical.

Getting your priorities in line can be tricky. I would even venture to say that it might be the single most difficult part about owning your own business or navigating your career. When you're so passionate about something, it's easy to dedicate your entire self to it. It's easy to think about it all day and all night. It's easy to forget about your social life, and I often find myself being pulled in so many different directions by my family, friends, and peers. People who work a 9-5 don't always fully understand that your 9-5 actually means "I don't stop working until my job is done." If I have something that needs to get done, I work until midnight, I (try to) wake up before the sun comes up, I give up wild nights out with my friends, I give up a lot of things that I see my friends doing on a regular basis. I'm not saying you need to give up doing anything social and fun 100%, but you will most likely find yourself doing those things considerably less than most people. Chasing your dreams requires a lot of sacrifice, especially in the beginning. The longer you play this game, the more comfortable you'll become with tuning out the party animals, the unmotivated people, the negativity, and shutting out anybody and anything that doesn't contribute to your success and well-being. **Live selfishly**.

When your goals are clear, your priorities are in line, and you have a fair amount of self-discipline, it may seem like your friends slowly start to trickle away. The ones who care about you, respect your hustle, and believe in you will stay by your side and respect your priorities. And you're lucky if you have friends that remain close to you even if you don't see them as often as you once did. For me, my best friend Mandy keeps my head on straight. As of right now, I have not seen her in nearly a year. And yes, I still consider her to be my best friend. She has a newborn baby and I have a four-year-old baby (my store), and we both respect how busy our lives are but we still text and communicate almost daily. We still tell each other our darkest secrets and of course gossip regularly.

Keeping your priorities straight and keeping yourself disciplined can prove to be the most difficult within your romantic life. I think friends are a little more forgiving than life partners are when it comes to time management. Your friends most likely have their own romantic lives and their own personal drama going on, so they don't expect to see you as often as a significant other does. I have mastered the art of keeping friends only by a few texts per week and occasional outings; however, this routine does not work with a spouse. I repeat, this routine does not work with a spouse. I feel like I almost don't even need to say this, but spouses obviously demand much more attention than friends do. And I can't blame them. That's how it should be in a relationship. You wouldn't date somebody or marry them only to expect to see them once every few months and exchange a few texts here and there. No. This is supposed to be your life partner. This is who you share everything with, spend each night with, and are expected to make them happy. Maybe it's just an entrepreneur thing but I find myself being extremely selfish with my time. Anybody else feel this way? This is either a blessing or a curse for me. Maybe a little bit of both.

Most every relationship that I've been in has consisted of the same general problem—not allocating my time properly. I wouldn't be the first person to call myself greedy with my time. When I wake up in the morning, the first thing I want to do is work. On my days off, I typically find myself working. And when I take extended vacations (which is rare), I often miss being at the shop and can't help but feel unproductive. Dinners with friends and family can prove difficult because somebody is always blowing my phone up about a piece of furniture or a sign getting completed. As the owner of a business with multiple moving parts, it can be hard to step away especially when you don't *want* to step away. Balance hasn't always been easy when it comes to dividing time between many important things and people.

Now, if we really want to get down to the nitty gritty of self-discipline, we can all especially relate on one particular topic… dieting! Am I right or am I right? For most of us, it's something that we have struggled with or at least been exposed to in some way. For me, my weight and physical appearance has been something that I've battled most all my life. In my younger years, I was always underweight. I was super self-conscious when it came to sports because most everything that I was involved in required you to wear short shorts or skirts, leaving my bird legs exposed.

During this time of my life, I was no stranger to youth group mission trips. I attended one most every summer, if not two. Mission trips are organized multi-day events where we volunteer to offer help where help is needed. For example, cleaning up after natural disasters, offering a helping hand at nursing homes, etc. Attendees of these trips were organized into age groups. Most often, they were divided by middle school and high school. So, I was always surrounded by people who were no more than one or two years in age difference; however, I was often the smallest of the bunch. I quickly became used to comments about anorexia and bulimia from my more "average-sized" peers. While eating disorders are not to be taken lightly, I can assure you that I was never a victim of one. Like I mentioned in my introduction, one of my biggest fears is throwing up and I honestly don't think I could make myself vomit if my life depended on it. Not to mention, I seriously love food y'all. I love food so much in fact that my eyes are normally larger than my stomach, meaning I have a habit of ordering more than I can usually eat in one sitting. Being on a mission trip, obviously you can't take your food "to-go" so there were a couple of times where I just threw away my leftovers on our way out. I should have known better, because how does that look? An underweight girl throwing away a cheeseburger with one bite taken out of it. The other kids on the trips wasted no time in ridiculing me about it.

As I got older, entering college, I was still the same ol' food-loving gal that I had always been. Except now, my metabolism was catching up with me. For the first time in my life, I was gaining weight. Gasp! I went from a mere 110lbs to roughly 150 in just about two short years. Now don't get me wrong, at 5'4", that's not overweight by any standards. But it was enough for me to notice that if I didn't start watching what I eat, it could easily escalate. Luckily my college roommate was what I would call a "gym rat", and she had me in the gym almost every day.

My weight and physical health in my adult life has never been anywhere near consistent and I recognize it as one of my flaws. I'm either really healthy or really not-so-much. For me, there's never been much of a gray area. One month, I'm eating fast food every night for dinner, and the next month I'm not even allowing myself to put dressing on my salad because I don't have room for "those 50 extra calories." Over the years, I've watched my weight fluctuate depending on my lifestyle and how motivated I'm feeling at the time. During the busier times of the year, I find it so easy to just pick up a cheeseburger on the way home. Certainly doesn't help that I live right down the road from Burger King. A cheeseburger with only mayonnaise, small fries, and some chicken nuggies... yes, please, don't mind if I do. Carving out time to grocery shop, cook food from scratch, and hit the gym has proven to be no easy task while running a small business full time.

It's only been in the recent year that I've found a decent balance. Through trial and error, I've found the only way to stay on track is literally just *force* it. My friends are all too familiar with this as I'm constantly the person telling them to stop making excuses. It's really simple to stop making excuses. Here's my big secret...

Just stop doing it.

Anyone can think of a million reasons not to go to the gym on any given day. Traffic is too bad, it's going to be crowded, I'm tired, I have other things to do. I don't want to hear it. If something is a priority in your life, which being healthy should be, then there's no excuse in the book that's good enough for me. Don't have time? Make time. Traffic is too bad? Leave earlier. As we've all heard before, "where there's a will, there's a way." This is my favorite saying that I like to use while trying to shove a bunch of furniture into a customer's car. If there is something in this life that you want, you will find a way to get it. After all, the only person in control of you is you. You decide what happens to your life, your schedule, and your body.

My advice to you would be to replace the phrase "I don't have time for that" with "that's not a priority." I guarantee it'll make you feel more guilty about not hitting the gym or following your dreams!

There is no reason why you *can't* do something. It's not that you don't have time, it's just that you aren't using your time in a way that creates the most growth. It's not that you don't have enough knowledge about a topic, you just haven't done enough research on it. And it's not that you don't have enough money, it's because you don't have the motivation to find a creative way to get the job done in an inexpensive way.

And let me tell you, if you think a lack of funds is the reason behind your failure to launch, then you are all kinds of twisted around. I'll clue you in on a little secret of mine. When I opened my first little boutique just about 4 years ago, my mom was paying for my groceries along with my apartment rent, I had about $50 in my bank account, and I made a whopping $300 on the "grand" opening day of my store. Ever heard the phrase "started from the bottom"? Yeah, that's me. I started from absolutely nothing, NOTHING!

"And let me tell you, if you think a lack of funds is the reason behind your failure to launch, then you are all kinds of twisted around."

Let's get real, I had no business opening a business (no pun intended), much less a brick and mortar store. In fact, I had every force in the world working against me at that time. I had no money, no business experience or schooling, and no inventory to sell. Not to mention my peers laughed at me whenever I brainstormed my idea aloud, and my parents weren't too happy about me not continuing on to get my master's degree in education. What I did have was a strong belief in myself and a whole lot of self-discipline. I found a reason and a way to overcome every single obstacle that was blocking my path. I turned down countless nights going out and doing the typical 'party girl" thing in trade for spending evenings at the shop working on renovations, talking to potential vendors to bring in, hunting for furniture, and other tasks that simply had to get done.

Again, the only person who's ever going to accomplish anything for you is you. You are given the same time and resources as each and every other person, if not more. It's your choice how to spend your 24 hours and 365 days. Discipline yourself.

Who you are when nobody else is watching

We could all use a little more of this. Google defines integrity as "the quality of being honest and having strong moral principles; moral uprightness." Yes, everybody's morals are going to be slightly different, but I would like to think that we can all agree that honesty is key, no matter what job title you hold.

I have found when dealing with my competitors, my customers, my co-workers, friends, family, peers, and with people who look up to me, honesty is the best policy.

I have always held myself to a very high standard when it comes to my integrity. My friends and family know that I often struggle with knowing what's right and what's wrong when it comes to difficult situations. I often find myself overly-stressing about the fear of doing the wrong thing. I'm not one to argue when I'm not 100% sure about something, but damn if I don't put up a fight when it's something that I strongly believe in.

There will be people constantly banging at your doors (figuratively and physically) trying to tell you which direction or side to take, what products or services to sell, what's good and not so good for you, how to make the most sales, and how to do your best advertising. The list could go on. There's a fine line between taking advice and letting somebody completely dictate your decisions.

If you haven't already started your business and its still basically just blueprints, now would be a good time to make some notes. Write down what you want to get from having your business – is it just a side hustle or do you want to make a living at it? This will help determine what you need (or don't need) before you begin. Make note of the things you want to sell or market and strategize a way to do it and stick with what you find works and ditch the things that don't catch on. I'm not saying don't ever take advice from anybody. I'll be the first to admit that I reach out to people for guidance when I feel stuck. But, be honest with yourself. Listen to what *you* want and stick to your guns. Don't let people talk you into doing certain things that your gut tells you isn't right. This goes for big decisions, but it also goes for small choices as well – things as small as where to place your greeting cards on your counter so that they appeal to the most customers.

I have found that in my line of work, there is always going to be somebody trying to bring me down or sabotage me. Whether it be little comments towards me here or there, saying something negative about my store to other people, or taking my sign down from out by the main road. Whatever it may be, there's always somebody out there doing or planning something petty. I have always chosen to take the high road and just say "bless your heart." I was taught to speak up when it matters, but to also know when to be the bigger person and keep my mouth zipped.

Being honest with yourself is important, but being honest with the outside world is also crucial. This doesn't mean that you have to answer every question that somebody asks you truthfully. There's always going to be people who want to poke and prod into your life. Some people are just nosey, some people are bored, and believe it or not there are always spies! Women love to talk and gossip. I always get asked odd questions, personal questions, and questions that I just downright don't want to answer. You don't have to lie to anybody. I normally just say that I don't want to talk about it or avert the conversation. And I don't feel bad about that. I got to the point where I had to create a "no gossiping" rule in my shop. And as I got older and stayed in business longer, I've also had to carry that rule into other places as well. You never know who you might run into and who's listening to your conversations. As my teachers would always say, "your character is who you are when nobody's looking."

It's always been extremely important to me to uphold my integrity, especially within my business because it helps to gain trust and loyalty from customers. I've often found my integrity being questioned when I'm faced with a tough decision. Instead of running from the problem, it's always better to face it head on and work to find a resolution. No matter what your job is, crisis is inevitable whether it be large or small. We've all had customers who've been disappointed in something that we've done, let's just admit it. When I first started my business, I was adamant that I would never disappoint anyone. Who was I kidding? I was naïve, but honestly, I did go about a whole year without hearing any complaints from anyone. It wasn't until I really started to grow that I finally got that one dreaded phone call. The delivery driver had just dropped off a newly painted bedroom set to my customer's home, which consisted of a couple of dressers and a nightstand. It was about thirty minutes after that when my phone began to ring. I had her phone number saved. So, when I saw her calling, naturally I quickly answered it in hopes that there weren't any issues upon delivery. What I heard on the other end of the line almost sent me into tears. There was yelling, there was attitude, there was confusion, and the occasional curse word spewing out of her mouth as word vomit. I stepped outside the back of my store and sat down in my paint-covered work chair. After a few deep breaths, I luckily managed to gather my thoughts and calm her down without a fight. She was dead-set on the fact that I painted her furniture using a different finish than what she had originally expressed an interest in. I assured her over and over that I did my absolute best, as always, and that if there were any discrepancies in the final product, it was surely due to a miscommunication somewhere along the line during our original consultation.

I may not have the best memory, but even to this day I can still vividly remember her pointing to and picking out the finish that she wanted done to these pieces, and this is *exactly* what I did on her dressers and nightstand. Maybe she was expecting it to look differently, maybe she was unsure of how this specific finish would look on a particularly large surface—who knows what the real issue was. Either way, she was very obviously unhappy with my work. And even though I had seen no wrongdoing, I immediately refunded her entire order.

As much as I hated to press that "send money" button, I knew I was saving myself from being badmouthed and possibly losing multiple customers. After receiving her refund, she called me again to let me know how pleased she was with my customer service and my willingness to fix the problem, assuring me that she would leave a five-star review on our Facebook page.

After running a retail store for a little over four years, I've listened to many customers complain about other stores' choices in handling problems. It's so easy to just immediately revert to your "all sales final" policy, but for me I also have a customer satisfaction policy and I've learned to lead with integrity even when it hurts.

Being able to use integrity to carry out personal morals and how the two tie together to create a reputation

I felt it fitting to put the morality and integrity chapter side by side as they work hand-in-hand. Integrity is used to carry out a person's morals. Although morals will vary from person to person, the importance of being able to stick to those morals does not. Or at least it shouldn't. Unfortunately, morality within business (small or large) is a huge controversy in today's world. Questions arise such as:

- What does morality matter as long as everybody is making money?
- What is really *good* for the company? And what does it mean to be "good" anyways?
- What does it really mean to be *successful*?
- Are you successful if you're profiting, but have to bend your morality in order to make it?

Business owners sometimes really struggle with knowing what their main focus is. Goals can oftentimes be blurred. Let's break it down. The notion that businesses prioritize money over moral values indicates the idea that the entity of business is totally separate from the human running it. They may have strict moral values when it comes to them as a human being, but when it comes to their business… not so much.

I sometimes have to remind myself; I am a SMALL business owner. And in the world of small business, you ARE the business. Your face is the face of the whole operation. There is no separation of you as a person from your job. It's all intertwined, and your customers are most likely going to know that. This is not so much the case when it comes to large chain stores. Most people don't know the person who's behind the scenes of businesses such as those.

A prime example of this is that most of my messages that come through to my One Rose Facebook page start out with "Hey Emily!" Even though I'm not always the one reading or responding to that message, the customer associates me with One Rose Decor at all times. Therefore, I keep a close eye on the moral values that I portray towards the business and my personal life. I pour my whole self into my business and in a large way, it's a direct reflection of me as a whole.

This is a topic that really hits home for me. Being so young when I first started, I never expected to see some of the things that I've seen in this small business world. People (women especially) can be downright evil towards each other and towards other businesses. It's a hard pill to swallow but you'll learn that not everybody is who they say they are. It's easy to assume that everybody wants good things for one another and that there's no ill intentions behind their generosity and good deeds. Unfortunately, that's not always the case. For some people, it's easy to kick aside their morals in order to take down the competition. Instead of getting offended by this, I remember that this is merely a sign of their weakness. I've learned that the people who bring others down instead of lifting them up are actually the most insecure of all. Those who try and make themselves seem "better" than everybody else are actually the ones who feel like they constantly have to prove themselves.

I've had to learn to stop questioning people's morality and just remind myself that it all boils down to insecurity. There wouldn't be a reason to sabotage another business if you didn't feel that they are a threat to you. I will repeat that...

There wouldn't be a reason to sabotage another business unless you feel that they were a threat to you!

It's not that these vultures don't have moral values. I'm sure they do. The difference between you and them is that they're willing to bend them and you're not.

Use your morals to attract customers! Once people realize how much of a great person you are, they'll always want to support you and your business. Kindness attracts kindness, and it draws people in. I don't know about you, but I love shopping at stores that are run by decent people who make me feel at home when I walk in. Nothing feels better than to support somebody who really deserves it. Not only will you attract more customers, but employees too.

You want good people to work for you and good people are only willing to work for other good people.

If you take nothing else from this book—a company's good reputation is their best asset. Dog ear the corner of this page or something but please don't let that sentence slip by you while reading this. Earning and keeping a good reputation with your followers is a vital way to use your integrity to uphold your personal morals.

The act of gaining more by giving more

I'll be the first to tell you that you get back what you give out. Maybe I'm just superstitious but I think karma is a real thing and let's be honest, don't we always want the good guy to win in the end?

I treat my regulars like family, and they do the same to me after a while. I know their names, I know what's going on in their lives, I meet their dogs (personally my favorite part of my job), and I can usually remember what items they've purchased from me over the years. I always greet each customer with a warm welcome, and typically I get the same in return.

My loyal customers are basically my bread and butter. I give back to them as often as I possibly can. By giving back, I mean free giveaways, drawings, raffles, discounts, etc. Yes, I set store policies and general business practices that I have to uphold such as return policies, etc. But I'll be the first to bend them when I feel it's necessary. The last thing I would want is a customer to leave the store unsatisfied or get home and realize that a shirt doesn't fit.

Give a random customer 10% off their purchase just because. Go ahead, do it. I'd be willing to bet my favorite paint brush that they'll be back next week to buy more. Or, if nothing else, they'll refer their friends and family to come see you. Word of mouth is everything when it comes to small business.

I never studied business in college. In fact, everything that I know about business and bookkeeping is self-taught. BUT, one thing I do know is how to work with people, and I know a whole heck ton about how to make sure that the customer always leaves the store happier than when they came in. And sometimes good people skills and knowledge of good customer service is all you need to get started and maintain a good reputation. Keeping good relations with the people in your life is key. Let me introduce you to Billy…

I was one year into owning my storefront when I met Billy. He was and still remains one of the most influential people in my life today. I was driving to work one morning when I noticed a massive yard sale out of the corner of my eye. It's not likely that I could drive past a yard sale without basically breaking my neck to see what they've got piled in their front yard for sale. *My apologies to the people who are driving near me on the road.* I distinctly remember an old heater covered in rust and two shutters appearing to be from the dinosaur age that caught my vintage-loving eyes as I pulled into the driveway. They were sitting right there on the front lawn. I was surprised nobody had snatched them up yet, but then again, some people would easily write those items off as trash.

I parked my car off to the side of the house and walked up. I was immediately greeted by a cheerful 70-something-year-old man. Snow white hair pulled back into a small ponytail, weighed maybe a generous 90lbs, and just a couple inches shorter than me. Very small man with lots of energy and full of stories. At this point, I knew I was going to be considerably late to work so I promptly called my mom and asked her favorite question "soooo…how much do you love me?" She usually responds with a long sigh and hesitantly asks me what I need. I asked her if she'd be willing to cover the store for me as the pickings were good at this pickin' sale and I knew I wasn't going to make it to work on time. As always, she was willing to cover the shop for me for an hour or two while I spent a good portion of my day digging through decades of "junk" in this man's garage.

I patiently listened to Billy tell me every detail behind each item that I was interested in (and some that I didn't even inquire about). He told me stories about countless pieces, some of which I heard two or three times before I finally left his house. I ended up leaving with a full truckload. He charged me a whopping five dollars for the entire haul. I laughed as I bungeed an old chippy door down to my dad's truck bed and told Billy how much I appreciated his generosity. He was clueless to the fact that this $5 haul was basically the highlight of my whole week. Nothing is more exciting than a good, inexpensive haul of new inventory for the shop.

Leaving his house that day, I had no idea that he would end up teaching me some of the most important lessons in life. His parents both passed away within the last couple of years and I know that sifting through all of their old belongings (and selling most all of it) must have been very difficult for him. I could tell that he found great joy in being able to share some of those treasures and stories with somebody who deeply appreciated them. Despite the pain and sadness he must have felt, he was nothing but grateful that I was there and that I could put these treasured things back to good use.

The items that I salvaged from that garage have a perfect home here at One Rose Décor and my customer's homes. There's a little bit of Billy all over the place here in Midlothian now.

Over the course of the following few years, I spent many hours hanging out with Billy, listening to stories about his childhood, fixing up old furniture, and sifting through his old family photos. We still can't figure out why people didn't smile in pictures back then—some of those old photos are just downright creepy. Even when I was short on time, I made time for moments like these with him. Even if it's just stopping by to say hello, I always made it a priority. If his beat-up pickup truck was in the driveway, I'd pull in. My time is not something that I can easily be generous with. In fact, I'm normally very selfish with my time because, well, time is money. But when it came to Billy, sharing my time came naturally. He deserved it. After all of his nice gestures, I felt the least I could do would be to spare my time and make the loss of his parents a little bit easier on him.

It's always a treat when he pops in the store for a minute or two. He always takes a couple unhurried laps around the store, pointing out all the items that I've bought from him and tells me how happy he is to see them cleaned up and on display. He typically ends the conversation with "you done good, kid!" and always leaves my heart feeling slightly fuller.

Now if you're anything like me, you've most likely been to your fair share of yard sales. More often than not, the seller is a little too "proud" of their items. $200 for an old rickety table? I don't think so!

On most occasions, I find myself walking around someone's front yard trying to wheel and deal in order to get a good price out of them, which ultimately leads to me leaving angry and the seller left with a yard full of "unsellables". But, Billy offered the kind of generosity that you don't find much of anymore in today's world. The kind of generosity where he expects absolutely nothing in return and always just wanted to make somebody happy.

Generosity is defined as "readiness or liability in giving" and being self-employed, I've become accustomed to doing a whole lot of giving in many different ways. If you aspire to grow your own company, build a brand, or simply start a side hustle, generosity is an aspect that can seem insignificant but often works in your benefit. First and foremost, as I mentioned earlier, is your time. Honestly, what is free time anymore? If you think being employed by yourself is a whole lot of "doing whatever you want," think again. Don't for a second underestimate the value in giving time to the people you work with, people who come to you for advice, and the good people you meet along the way. You never know who could open doors for you, or who's door you could open.

Forgiveness

Stuff happens.

I know what you're thinking. This chapter doesn't belong in this book, right? Wrong. The more I think about forgiveness and the more I write about it, the more I actually love it. And I'm not talking about forgiving others, I'm talking all about forgiving *yourself.* Making mistakes is a difficult thing for those of us who are extremely hard on ourselves. We must learn to relentlessly eliminate unforgiveness from our lives for one simple reason: to grow.

If you own a business, no matter how big or small, chances are you're probably very hard on yourself. As entrepreneurs, we are hardwired to make careful, calculated decisions, and we want to be the very best version of ourselves. We jump into things full force and go after our dreams full speed ahead. So, when things don't go as planned it's easy to feel the need to beat ourselves up. After all, we are our own worst critics.

Our gut tells us what the right thing is most of the time, but what about when it doesn't point us in a clear direction? I've grown to know the importance of self-forgiveness for my not-so-great choices. If you're anything like me, you take your sweet time to make decisions. Nothing happens for me without taking into consideration every possible outcome and heavily weighing the pros and cons. I undoubtedly stress myself out more than I should.

When you finally come to the realization that you're in control of your own life, it can feel like there's a lot riding on you. It sometimes feels like the weight of the world on your shoulders and especially as a business owner, you wear multiple hats. When something doesn't go as planned, it's nobody's fault but our own (no pressure or anything!).

It's difficult to make sense of situations when they don't pan out the way you had expected. How could I possibly think so hard about something and then have it end up not working out? Just because you're your own boss, doesn't mean you have the right answers all the time. You are a smart, brilliant, passionate, and driven... but sometimes you will be *wrong*. Learning how to forgive yourself will ultimately give you freedom. With the mindset that you can recover from anything, you'll quickly realize that anything is possible. Some of my most carefully thought-out decisions have been the worst things for me. Remember that time I moved my retail store in next door to a dance studio? I was still in that space when I started writing this paragraph actually. Thank goodness I have since moved and can actually finish writing without having to listen to Irish dance music on repeat. Let me see a show of hands from all of my regulars who know all too well what I'm referring to! I know y'all can hear it in the back of your heads right now... shoes endlessly tapping the dance floor and pounding music while you're trying to browse my cozy, not-so-peaceful boutique.

"With the mindset that you can recover from anything, you'll quickly realize that anything is possible."

When I moved into that store originally, I made a pros and cons list. It had exactly what I needed... concrete floors that I was allowed to get paint on, a garage door, beautiful bay window in the front, a utility sink for all of my messiness, a garage for me to paint in... the works! It's perfect, right? Wrong. Apparently "we only practice in the evenings" actually means "we will only be practicing during the day during your store hours." Obviously, I should have done my homework and made multiple visits to this location before signing the lease. Like I said, sometimes we don't have all the right answers and I hate to say it, but sometimes our gut will let us down.

Looking back, despite the loud incessant stomping, I'm still immensely thankful for the year and a half that I spent there. That little space was the steppingstone that I needed to push me to my next career move and into a bigger and more efficient storefront. There were many days I spent beating myself up for signing that lease. At 8:00am, I longed to start my day with a cup of coffee and some motivational music. I'm a firm believer in that how you start your day will set the tone for the rest of the hours to come. Beginning my day with some sunrise stomping and morning madness coming from next door really put a damper on things for me on a regular basis. I was unable to focus or finish a project. And being able to stay in a good mood all day long? Yeah, you could forget about that.

There were days when I would question what I was doing, questioned the choices I had made, and mostly questioned my own judgment. Frankly, I was beating myself up for overlooking such an important factor when signing a lease to a storefront. The end of my career could have very well been there in that little shop if I had allowed it to come to that.

All you can do is learn from your mistakes. There's no point in beating yourself up about them. If you love what you do and you feel in your heart that you're on the right path, you *will* keep on keepin' on. I've learned the hard way that you can't let bad choices cause you to lose faith in yourself. Honestly, I like to think that there are no such things as "bad" choices. There are only choices that have led you to get where you are now. If I hadn't moved into that steppingstone store, I wouldn't have been able to get into the much larger location that I'm in now. It was a much-needed baby step.

I sometimes spend months contemplating whether or not to do something and often refer to other people for advice. I'm an open book and I'll tell anybody what's on my mind at any given time. Having said that, when something does go right, it's the most rewarding experience and I always give myself a pat on the back. You can't forget to praise yourself when it's called for! Brace yourself, small business (and especially retail) is such a roller coaster ride. Forgiveness is imperative if you desire a forward movement in your personal life as well as within your small business.

Have I let my mistakes make me think less of my judgment calls? A little bit, but will I let this stop me from moving forward? No way in hell, which leads me to our next trait, persistence...

persistence

Whatever you do, DO. NOT. STOP.

Often, when I'm scrolling through Pinterest for inspirational quotes, I always seem to stumble upon the same one time and time again: "The best things are usually about to happen when you feel like you're at your lowest point." After all, there's only one way to go when you're at the bottom, and that's up. I didn't always believe this until life proved it to be correct.

After neighboring that dance studio for about a year and a half, I had finally just signed the lease to my new dream store, but I had 2 months of renovations ahead of me before I would be able to officially open my shop in that new location. This meant I had two months ahead of me where I would have to juggle still running my store full time while also renovating 3,500 square feet at the new place. No big deal! After difficulties with my landlord, the constant stomping next door, and a horrible breakup with my ex who had been a significant part of my business up until that point, let's just say I was more than ready to put this old place behind me. I was more than ready to make that place a part of my past and get all settled in at the new store. A fresh start. My team and I had quickly outgrown that space, I sank money into building repairs that should have been the landlord's responsibility, and quite frankly I was just excited to start this new chapter in a much larger space, free of Irish dance music.

After signing the new lease, I could hardly wait to get my hands on it and moved in. In order to keep the number of items we had to move to a bare minimum, all new inventory that came in during this two-month period went straight to the new store. That way we wouldn't have to move it twice. This meant that Huguenot (the old store) was looking beyond sparse and messy. Customers were so excited about the grand opening at the new space that they stopped shopping at Huguenot altogether. During the last few weeks, there was hardly any inventory to browse! I was losing motivation…fast, which is something that is unheard of for me. There were a couple days that I left work heading home in tears. I couldn't bring myself to find the fire within me to create or paint anything. I was tired and I felt like I wasn't using my time properly. If you know me personally, you know that my biggest pet peeve is wasting time. I was over it.

My plan was to stay open for business at Huguenot right up until only 3 days before the grand opening of the new and improved location; however, it quickly became apparent that I wasn't going to last that long. Things were growing slower and slower there at Huguenot and all that I was itching to do was work on the renovations at Grove to make it perfect. My time could definitely be put to better use.

I decided to close Huguenot a few days earlier than I had originally planned. I wanted to put the pedal to the metal in the new store. The last day that I was open for business at Huguenot was also the day that I had to put down my childhood dog, Beatrice. Needless to say, I had completely hit a wall of depression at this point when it was all said and done. I was so absolutely worn out from working full days and then working on renovations through the nights. I was, for lack of a better term, a hot mess on that last day of work.

I began to wonder… what if I can't navigate my way out of this mental funk? What if I can't find the motivation to do these renovations correctly and to the best of my abilities? It was in those few days of depression that I came across that quote once again. I tried to internalize it and believe in myself the way I always have. I knew I was at one of my lowest points both physically and mentally and I knew that it should only get better from that point on.

It was the very last day of grabbing all of my remaining things from the old store. A dear friend of ours offered to rent a moving van and lend a helping hand with getting it all out, thank goodness. Finally, after what felt like an eternity, I stood there in that empty space waiting for one last customer to show up and grab something from me that she had purchased online. I rolled around in what was the last piece of furniture still left in there, my beloved rolly chair salvaged from a nearby elementary school. I swiveled around and scrolled through my phone as I waited, finally catching a peaceful moment. Rae (my customer) pulled into the parking lot. I greeted her as she walked in, just as I always had. She gave me a hug and before I could hand over her purchase, she handed me a card. It was a card with a little love note about the loss of my 18-year-old dog, Bea, which had been obviously weighing heavy on my mind. I gave her a longer-than-normal hug and told her "thank you" countless times. I waited to open the card until I got home, as I knew I wouldn't be able to hold back tears in front of her. I may be able to say and do anything else in front of people, I'm an open book, but you won't catch me crying! We chatted briefly about the move and about Bea, and then we loaded up her goodies into the back of her car, and off she went.

To me, this was such an unexpected glimmer of hope and comfort in a time where I so desperately needed it. I saved that card. It's still in the top drawer of my cabinet in my living room. I don't know about you guys, but I always keep greeting cards, especially the ones with little handwritten messages on them. Call me old fashioned. I actually had it hanging up on my fridge for the entire remainder of the renovation process in honor of Bea, but also just as a reminder that things will get better.

With a little (or a lot) of coffee, countless weeks of setting up and decorating the new store, cutting all ties with the old store at Huguenot, I finally felt like I was back on track. Despite the many times I've questioned being self-employed, resented the hard work that comes with it, and just felt straight up TIRED, none of those horrible feelings can even compare to how amazing it feels to be able to live-out your passions, your dreams, and your ambitions.

While on the topic of persistence, let's talk about my panic attacks. Something that so many women in my circle suffer from or have at least experienced. I've always pictured myself as a fairly mentally strong person, and then my first panic attack came along with a big ol "heck naw, honey!" I mean, it hit me like a ton of bricks. My heart rate rose to a point where I couldn't catch my breath, my hands started shaking, and then the nausea set in. Thirty minutes or so passed by before I started pacing. Back and forth, back and forth down the hallway of my friend's hallway as he sat on the couch completely invested in his video game. I had no idea what was going on, so naturally what do I do? Call my mom!

Out of all of my drunken college nights, I somehow survived on my own. Drunk, wobbly, giggly Emily surviving the Richmond house parties and yet here I am on this particular night calling for my mom to rescue me because of literally no reason at all. That's what killed me the most about struggling through panic attack after panic attack was that I couldn't find a reason behind them. I'm not exaggerating when I say I spent years of my life trying to find a REASON. At 22 years old, I had not yet endured the loss of a pet, close loved one, a breakup, nothing. Why was I panicking? Why was my anxiety through the roof? Soon, searching for the reason behind my debilitating anxiety became worse than the actual anxiety itself. I was having anxiety about anxiety, as ridiculous as that sounds.

At one point, I thought to myself, I wouldn't mind if one of these panic attacks killed me. I literally felt like dying would be better than continuing to experience that.

You know, there's been many occasions in my life where Applebee's has been the cure. Yes, you read that correctly. A nice big plate of buffalo chicken strips piled over top of an unhealthy amount of cheese-drenched pasta. Get in my belly! My panic attacks have always come at the most random and often inconvenient times. In this particular case, I had just sat down with a friend for dinner and I felt it. It was coming. Coming for me like Mother Nature hitting you while in a white bikini.

Now, if you know me, you know that I often struggle to find time to spend with my friends. So, the fact that I was actually out to dinner with one was an actual miracle. I was absolutely not about to let this ruin my one night out. No way, no how. I wasn't in the comfort of my home (or my mother's passenger seat). I was out in public, surrounded by people. I know I'm quite capable of causing a scene but I really wanted to avoid that on this night. *God, please just let me enjoy this one night out and get through it with ease and peace.* This night went down in history as one of the very first times that I really pushed through something mentally and came out on the other side. Yay me! I literally thought my way out of the negative energy that was trying to rain down on me. I pushed those vibes away so forcefully that I could actually feel my knuckles turning white from clenching my fists so tightly and secretively under the table. Before I knew it, I was sucked into a conversation with my friend, laughing and talking, and not a worry in the world.

We are capable of anything, literally anything. Fear is only that, fear. There is nothing that we are actually scared of. What we're actually afraid of is the feeling of fear itself. Imagine the happiness that would come as a result of mentally pushing away the fears that we conjure up in our brains. Fear simply stems from the possibility of being uncomfortable.

And let me tell ya, nothing can make you feel more uncomfortable than a world-wide health pandemic raining (storming) down on your parade. A small business's worst nightmare.

Just one short week after opening our in-store cafe Spring 2020, COVID-19 strikes. First order of business: shut down all restaurants and eateries. Thank goodness we sold out of all our food during our grand opening because starting the following day, it was peace out pies and sianara scones!

While the majority of the world is at home making TikTok videos, sewing face masks, and over-washing their hands, small businesses everywhere were scrambling. How will the bills get paid? Will people still be shopping? Am I allowed to even stay open?

I open up a Word document and type up what every business owner hopes to never have to say; "CLOSED until further notice" and hesitantly scotch-taped it to my store window. Aside from that, I was going to have to type up not only an explanation but also a solution (which was nonexistent at the time) on my private vendor page on Facebook as to why none of their items were going to sell this month. This is the private group where my vendors, employees, and I can chat about things going on around the shop, sales, etc. Twenty-eight consignors were waiting to see what our plan was. Truth was, I didn't have one.

I left the shop closed for two full days in hopes that this would all blow over. Hi, my name is Emily, and my optimism gets the best of me. This couldn't last long, could it? At the end of day two with little-to-no sales, I decided to open the store to customers on the basis of appointment only, which was great, but my golden ticket was ultimately the internet. I sat down at my checkout counter and hastily posted 7 cyber events to our store's Facebook page. One for each day of that week. Normally there's countless hours of thought and graphic design trial and error behind our event postings, but not this time. Each event was created in about 5 minutes, complete with spelling errors and everything! There's no time to waste y'all, we are in the midst of a pandemic! From the looks of it, this thing was going to last a whole lot longer than we anticipated and I had 28 vendors relying on me to make sales and my apartment complex waiting for me to pay my rent. It was pedal to the metal... cyber style! We took One Rose to the internet and to the comfort of our customer's couches.

I spent the better part of 2 months being on my phone. Family events, on my phone. At a friend's house, on my phone. Talking to a customer, on my phone. So very sorry to those of you who had to hold a conversation with me while I was nose deep in my screen.

Posting items, sending invoices, making a sale, packaging, shipping, answering messages, sleeping (occasionally), REPEAT! Those few weeks were a whirlwind and I'm still not fully convinced that it wasn't all a dream. April 2020; the month of excessive hand washing and second highest grossing sales month ever to exist for our store. To put it in perspective, our sales that month were comparable to what we normally pull during December around Christmas time. Insanity! And 75% of it was done through the internet. Who would have thought?

I've said it before, and I will say it again: Stop finding reasons why not to. Multi-million-dollar chain stores, movie theaters, and restaurants were closing indefinitely due to this virus. We had every reason in the world to think we wouldn't come right-side-up after the air *literally* cleared. We had every right to panic and think the worst (and I did a lot of that). They say where there's a will, there's a way. There I go with the overused quotes again, but it's true. If you want something bad enough, not even a world-wide pandemic can stop you from doing what you have to do in order to keep a roof over your head and your "open" sign on.

originality

Be a flamingo in a flock of pigeons

Somebody once told me that true inspiration does not exist, meaning that even when you think you've come up with a brand-new idea on your own, chances are that your idea probably stemmed from something you've already seen or heard, whether you know it or not. Your brain is stimulated by so many different things on a daily basis, more than we can even fathom. And when you add up all the days that you've lived during your life…yeah, that's a lot of stimulation and countless things that you've seen and experienced and may not remember.

Genuine inspiration has to come from within yourself. Instead of grasping ideas and business models from others, we need to find motivation from being in love with our own journeys. Use your actions, your thoughts, and your passion to fuel your fire and have the courage to be totally obsessed with who you are. Think about it, not one of us is ever made the same. We each have our own voice, talents, interests, and desires. What's the point of striving to be like another person or do the same thing as someone else when you can be *you*? You can and will do things that no other person has ever done. The world needs you!

When creating something new for my store, I think *have I seen this done before?* I dig deep, *have I even seen something relatively similar*? I try to create new inventory just by using ideas from my own imagination but let me tell you, it's not as easy as it sounds. In today's world, and especially in the crafting world, there are so many ideas that have already been taken. But if there's one thing that you should never forget, it's to make sure you are always different from your competitors, even in the smallest ways. I know sometimes with crafting, it can almost feel like you're trying to reinvent the wheel. We live in the age of Pinterest, a whole online world of ideas just waiting for you to try them all.

Don't get me wrong, you still probably want to keep up with current trends. Know what your customers want and what they're looking for but put your own spin on it. Make it your own.

No successful business runs off somebody else's business model. Hate to break it to you, but you will fail, embarrassingly, if that's the route you try to take. And trust me, stealing ideas doesn't go unnoticed. Some may think they can pull it off.

Maybe if I'm extra stealthy about it, nobody will notice.

Maybe if I just don't put my name on my price tag, nobody will blame me.

Maybe if I just make it an inch or two bigger than hers or change the color slightly.

Errrr! Wrong!

Always assume that everybody is watching you, and honestly, they probably are. If you have competition, they *are* watching. And not just your competitors but also your customers, your supporters, your peers, and the people who look up to you as well. They're watching, and they're analyzing your moves. Some of them want nothing but failure for you, but some of them also want to see you succeed.

I was once told by a dear family friend to always act as if you could suddenly be interviewed at any point in time. I think about this often when it comes to the direction that I take my business, the way I dress (even though you can usually find me in a painting T-shirt and a messy bun), and the decisions that I make regarding myself as well as One Rose.

"So, Ms. Hubbard, tell me about this product that you created."

What are you going to say? You certainly wouldn't tell them that you stole the idea from another business, would you? Would you lie and make up a story about how you thought up the idea on your own? I would like to think that we are all a little bit better than that!

And let me tell you, people TALK. Lord, people talk. I'm going to assume that the majority of my readers are women, so let's just be real, we gossip. We do! So even when you aren't keeping up with the competition, you will hear about them from other people whether you want to or not. Point is, stolen ideas do not slip under anybody's radar.

Currently being one of the youngest people in this game, I've relied on lots of my older boss babes to provide me with advice and guidance when needed. One of my most trusted fellow business owners once told me to think about your journey as a bike race. Picture yourself on the track, ten other riders to your left. Ten other riders to your right. You're all riding within just a couple inches of each other. What happens if you look to your left, even just slightly? Your wheel is slightly going to start to angle to the left, you're going to lose your balance, and you're going to crash. And not only are you going to crash, but everybody else who's behind you is going to ride straight around you without pause. Not to mention, everybody standing in the crowd just witnessed this. Yikes.

For goodness sakes, put some blinders on! Put them there and do not touch them. Do not take them down for any reason. If you don't pay attention to others beside, behind, or in front of you, you have no way of knowing what they're doing or in which direction they're headed. Stay in your lane, focus on *your* path, and keep those blinders on. I know there's no chance of me accidently "ripping off" somebody

135

else's product if I am fully focused on myself and my own ideas.

Without even a single doubt, the best and healthiest thing I've ever done for myself is unfollow my competitors on social media. I would even venture as far as to say that this might be one of the most vital and truest paragraphs in this entire book. Social media can be a total whirlpool. You get on your phone, click on something which leads you to click on something else, and then before you know it, you're stalking the Facebook profile of a person that you don't even know! I guess curiosity and spare time are to blame for this, but nevertheless, it's the most unproductive way to utilize precious time.

Being a startup business in the technology age, you could say it's been fairly easy to establish a large social media following for my business, which has been a good thing for sales but a not-so-good thing for the world of competition. Every which way I turn, I see another similar business popping up. Don't get me wrong, I'm all for women following their passions and carrying out their dreams, but it's not exactly ideal to see what they're doing every time I hop online. After unfollowing my competitors, blocking the ones who I've had bad relations with, and unfriending the personal pages of the owners, my entire life changed. Dramatic, huh? But it's the truth. Not only did I feel happier after becoming unaware to what they were up to, I also felt 100% completely and unapologetically FREE. All of a sudden, I was the only one in the game, totally immersed in the brand I was building and not worried about what anyone else was doing.

But of course, if somebody gets very visibly in your lane to the point where they are blocking you from your own success, set them straight. Let me elaborate a little more on that.

I'm not one to enjoy confrontation at all. In fact, I do everything I possibly can to avoid it. I've spent the last 3 months listening to the guy who lives below me play pounding music non-stop because I literally refuse to go down there and say something to him. *Who needs peaceful sleep, right?* It's just my style—I keep to myself; however, when it comes to my business, I don't let too many things go.

I treat my business as my baby. Here I have this thing, this entity, that I have created. I've built it from the ground up. It's so precious to me. It's always my gut instinct to protect it with everything I have, whatever the cost may be. For me, in this scenario, the cost was my reputation in the eyes of a few people. It was kind of heartbreaking for me because I hold my reputation as a businesswoman to a very high standard at all times.

I had just hosted my very first big Valentine's Day open house at my store. I was so proud of all of the items that we had for sale and the perfectly curated displays that were put together. My vendors and artisans had really brought their A-game for this sale. *Here's a virtual high five if you're a 1R vendor reading this.* I carefully watch the products that come into my store for sale because I don't want anything in here that I believe is "overdone" or that people have already seen made a hundred times before at other local stores. I have faith in my vendors that they use their own creative juices to create their items rather than pulling ideas from others. And I know personally that I had created a line of gorgeous wooden signs for this event. I hadn't gotten this idea from anywhere on the internet or from another store. They were totally original to me and to One Rose. They had a white background, black text, and pink trim (rarely do I paint with pink, but I thought it would make them super unique and one of a kind just for this specific sale). I was so proud of what I had created and knew they would sell immediately, which they did.

It was only about one month later that I found the exact, and I mean EXACT, same signs in another local store. Price tags even had basically my same name on them (only one word was different from mine). I won't disclose that name, but I can assure that it would have easily been confused with my store name by any customer who would have glanced at them.

For a minute I just stood there examining the product. *No way these are mine. No way somebody actually bought this from my store and then put it up for sale here.* But an artist can always recognize their own work after looking at the details. They were not the signs that I had made but to an everyday customer, they might as well have been. They were identical to what I had created and sold just one month earlier, down to every last detail. Even the price and size were the exact same as mine.

I was shopping with my mom on this particular day and she was looking at some items in the room next to me. I quickly called her in and showed her the knockoffs. My mom isn't as hot-headed as I am and rarely do she and I have the same reactions to things. She is usually more mellow and I'm usually more "OMG!" But even she was a little freaked out by what she saw. I tried to let it go. I thought it was weird, even thought it was a little concerning, but it wasn't the end of the world, right?

Shortly after this, she strikes again! Original products from One Rose were being ripped off at an astonishing and almost unbelievable rate. We would post a new item on our Facebook page and a couple days later a knockoff version would be posted on their Facebook page. It was the weirdest thing. It would be easy to assume this was just a coincidence if these products were easily found on Pinterest or if they were very generic, but they weren't! These were items that we had custom made and designed ourselves. In other words, these creations were totally original to our store.

Again, I just let it go.

It wasn't until I started receiving messages from other store owners alerting me that they were noticing what was going on and to be cautious. I'd like to think that most people who own their own store (or business owners in general) have pretty level heads, but I guess there will always be exceptions, so

I started compiling information. I was saving pictures and dates onto my phone. At the time, I wasn't planning on taking any action. I just wanted to have all of my information organized in case I really did have to confront somebody.

The messages and warnings kept coming in. Soon after that, a few of my vendors came to me and began telling me about how this other store owner was messaging them and trying to convince them to leave my store and come sell in their store instead. Steal my ideas and then steal my vendors ideas as well?! *Oh, hell no.* I finalized the album on my phone and finally confronted the owner of the store. Of course, she immediately took offense to it and probably still to this day isn't very fond of me. But, as far as I know, the 1R duplicate products ceased to exist afterwards. And at the end of the day, that's all I wanted. Maybe they thought I was just flattering myself and being arrogant, but I always do what I think is right. I think most anyone can vouch that I'm not a harmful or rude person, but I will always protect my store as if it's my baby.

Look, there's going to be haters, there's going to be copycats, there's going to be people who downright don't even like who you are as a person, but we can't please everyone. Even if you looked EXACTLY the way you want to look, I'm talkin' no cellulite, no stretch marks, gorgeous hair, there's still going to be somebody out there who finds something about you that they deem ugly. No matter how great I stage my store or how I interact with other business, there will always be another business looking down on me. We can't allow this negativity to keep us from being us! After all, the easiest thing to be is, well, yourself! I mean really, it takes zero effort to just do, create, act, say, the things that you *want* to!

Imagine this. A life where you didn't care what anybody thought of you. And when I say, "imagine this", I really want you to picture it because mindlessly reading words on a page doesn't do anybody justice, so get with the picture! You can't honestly sit there and tell me that you wouldn't be doing at least one thing differently. If we did everything, literally everything, without considering the opinions of others, our lives would completely change.

What's that one outfit in your closet that you bought and never wore because you were too afraid of what people might think? Just because it's a little bit different than the current "fashion trends." We all have one. We tried on some high waisted pants at TJ Maxx and thought they made our butt look really good and our thighs nice and toned. *Damn you fantastic lighting in the fitting rooms*. They're super-flare bellbottom jeans and they'll pair perfectly with a cute tank top you have at home. Chic, right?

Then, the reality of your home mirror strikes! Your thighs all of a sudden don't look as great and *who wears bellbottoms nowadays anyways*? Suddenly, you're not so brave and your J-Lo booty doesn't look so J-Lo-ish anymore in your mind. You fold them back up and quickly store them in the bottom of your dresser drawer only to collect dust for the next year. For the next couple of months, you continue wearing the same old jeans that you're "comfortable" in. These are your no-risk, safe jeans. You know, the ones that suppress your inner fashion queen.

Now, not everyone's originality comes in the form of fashion. That's the beauty of originality! For some it may be music taste, personality, career paths, or a mixture of all of the above. Whatever it is, try picturing yourself embracing all of those things without wondering or caring what anybody else thinks. It. Is. Life-changing.

Let me tell you one thing, there is not one person that I look up to who isn't unique. Not a single soul. None of my role models are cookie cutter humans and cookie cutter humans wouldn't even exist if we were just all living without the need to please others.

innovation

It's not just about ideas.
It's about making those ideas happen!

Innovation is what we use to put our originality to work. I was in business for almost 3 years before I made the best decision that I've ever made as a business owner. Teaching calligraphy was not how my business started off. In fact, it wasn't even a thought that had crossed my mind at all at the time. When I founded One Rose Décor in 2015, I was strictly doing furniture painting. This was right at the time where it seemed like every single person in the state of Virginia was catching onto the DIY furniture painting trend. I knew that I needed to do something to set myself apart.

It wasn't until one of my clients asked me if I made signs, that I had even considered signage as something I was capable of. Of course, I immediately said no. I couldn't charge a customer for a product that I had no idea if I was even capable of making or not. But I thought about it every day for months after that. It wasn't until another person inquired about the possibility of purchasing a hand-lettered sign that I finally decided to at least give it a try. I have a real problem saying "no" to customers and to people in general, which has been a blessing and a curse. On the one hand, it feels really great to be able to avoid doing things that I don't want to do, but on the other hand taking risks and doing projects outside of my comfort zone has sometimes led me down amazing paths that I never would have expected.

I bought my first paint pen having no clue what I was looking at. It was a brand that I would never recommend to anybody now that I actually know what I'm doing. I sat down with this piece of wood, my crappy paint pen, and just stared at it feeling like a fish out of water. I sketched it out in pencil first, making sure that I was allowed to make mistakes, then finished it off with paint pen and clear coat. At the time, I saw the finished product as being equivalent to the Mona Lisa. It was fantastic—the best thing I've ever done! (Even though it really wasn't.)

I remember it as if it was yesterday, I texted my friend and sent a picture of the masterpiece that I had just completed. I said something along the lines of, "why don't I do this for a living?!" To which they responded, "well then do it!" That was that. I was on the road to being one of the only people to offer calligraphy classes in the Richmond, Virginia area. I've now been teaching calligraphy workshops and offering custom lettering for just over three years and it has become the signature of One Rose. Who would have ever guessed?

In my workshops, my favorite thing to hear is "wow, I've been looking for something like this for so long. I'm so glad I found you." And that, my friends, is the type of comment that I strive so hard to hear. Whether it be a physical product, an idea, a design, or a service that you're offering, the key is that your consumer can't find it elsewhere (at least not easily or at the same price).

I work day-in and day-out to make sure that our quaint little store here in Midlothian isn't your typical shopping experience. I've carefully curated the building so that our customers are still able to see the remnants of the 1940s when it was originally a motel. While some other potential tenant might have come in and not appreciated that aspect of the building, I always have. The history of the building is something that I wouldn't trade for the world. When you enter through our front door, you are immediately greeted with photos of the motel from the 40s as well as treasures that have been salvaged and up-cycled to meet 2020. Within every twist and turn, you are guaranteed to find something that you've never seen before.

I have been so blessed to have customers who can appreciate our style and uniqueness throughout our store and who have been so receptive to all the new and innovative ideas that I've introduced into the store over the past few years. One man's trash is another man's treasure.

Through trial and error, here are some tips that I have found that keep me feeling sharp and full of new ideas:

1. Get off your phone! Don't run to Pinterest to find ideas when you're not feeling motivated or inspired. Put your phone away and out of sight. Instead, get your inspiration

from the outdoors or through doing other activities.

2. Stand up! This might sound weird since you're probably exhausted from working your butt off all the time. Why stand when I don't need to? Heck, I've laid in bed most of the time that I've spent writing this book. But your creative juices flow better when you're standing. Not sure how to put that into scientific terms to make it more believable, but how about just take my word for it? If you have a stand-up chalkboard, easel or dry erase board, that would be perfect. Grab a pen, paint brush, chalk or whatever utensil you're most comfortable with and just start brainstorming. One of my favorite ways to organize my thoughts is to make webs, maps, and outlines. Brainstorming is most likely going to be different for all of us. For some, its writing. For others, it's drawing. Whatever it is, just get up and find something that works for you.

For me, I also like to talk to other people during this process. Just before big store events, I like to run my ideas by other people (even if they have no retail knowledge and really have no idea what I'm talking about). It just helps me to get my thoughts flowing. I end up coming up with ideas that I didn't even know I had stored in this brain of mine.

3. Another helpful tip when trying to be innovative is to ban certain things. Might sound counterproductive at first, but it all depends on what exactly you're planning to ban. Think about what's toxic to you and your business. Sometimes, these can actually be things that we like or enjoy. Think about what's been most helpful to you. For me, like I said, it's my phone. I have to put my phone away or I'll find myself 40 weeks deep on somebody's Instagram page or lost in the bowels of Pinterest. It's terrible. I turn on my King Princess Pandora station, hook it up to

my Bluetooth, and leave it alone for the next couple hours. I refuse to look at it until I've finished the task at hand or at least get to a stopping point. I find that's when my brain seems to work the best. I call this my "zone" and we all have one. My zone tends to be rather obnoxious since I like my music so loud. Sorry neighbors. Another thing that may be helpful for you to ban would be watching TV while trying to brainstorm. We all love to watch Chip and Joanna but let's be honest, we won't get anything done while watching them. Tune all that out… focus.

4. Start small. It can be extremely intimidating and overwhelming to think about how you can skyrocket your business from the get-go. Especially if you are just starting out. If you're new to the small business game, it's counterproductive to think about those things right away. Start small and trust the process. The big ideas will hit you when you're least

expecting them. In the meantime, think little. Focus on the things that your gut tells you to focus on and I can assure you that you'll be on the right path. Those small ideas and events here and there will lead you right to where you're supposed to be, and the big game-changers will happen along the way when you least expect it.

Perseverance

You didn't come this far,

to only come this far

Persistence in doing something despite
difficulty or delay in achieving success. This doesn't
come easy for a lot of us because the only way to
build it up, is to get knocked down and endure a few
setbacks. I use the term "setbacks" instead of
"failures" because failure implies that the journey is

over. If you fail at something, it's essentially done. Adios, ka-put. "Setback" implies that you've simply hit a minor speedbump. A hitch in the ole' giddy-up as I like to say. The more setbacks you overcome, the more you build your resilience. To do so, you must fully commit to a forward movement, like we talked about earlier. Setbacks must be viewed as learning experiences rather than a final curtain draw. To be quite frank… shit happens! I like to put my big girl pants on, get over it, and keep truckin'. There is absolutely nothing and no one who can stop me once I'm committed to something.

I'm a firm believer that everything happens for a reason. Or at least reason can be *found* in everything. There's a timeline that we are each supposed to follow, and we have to trust it. If something doesn't work out, it's only because there's something better waiting for you right around the corner. I can't even begin to count the many opportunities that have been presented to me that I didn't take. Some of those opportunities didn't pan out because I didn't allow them to, but others didn't work out because of reasons that were beyond my control.

"If something doesn't work out, it's only because there's something better waiting for you right around the corner."

When I first opened my store back in 2016, I was in what I like to call my "starter store." It was just enough to get me up on my feet and get my name out there. It was tiny, but it was cute, all 200SF of it. During that first year, what kept me motivated was making sure I stayed focused on my long-term goals. I always had a vision in the back of my head of what I wanted my store to be in the long run and I was willing to stop at nothing to get there. I dreamt of an old, historic building with all original features and lots of character. I thought I would never find it…

until I did. There it was, sitting right off of a main road. All three stories of it standing tall, almost taunting me as I drove by. At the time, this particular building wasn't even for sale. I stalked it for a while just to see what it was being used for. I never saw cars in the parking lot and there was no sign on the building itself. Its mystery is partially what drew me in. I spent weeks doing some not-so-creepy surveillance on the building. You know, just peeking in through the windows after dark and circling the building in my car during the day. Casual. I finally discovered who owned it and with the help of my dad, we got in contact. Discovering that it had no permanent use, we decided to offer an unsolicited proposal to the owners.

We composed a letter of interest. I thought of every reason in the book why it would be better off in the hands of One Rose Decor. Why not sell it to somebody who will love it, treasure it, and maintain its integrity? We took multiple tours of the building. My dad and I analyzed every square inch of it and just as expected, I fell head over heels. I needed it. I was convinced that it was made for me. The original hardwood floors, tin ceiling, and a hundred-year-old elevator tunnel were absolutely drool-worthy. This building had endured decade after decade of multiple uses just to get to this point where I would purchase it and turn it into One Rose Décor's permanent home.

I know, I'm really hyping you guys up to believe that this actually worked out.

They gave me about 6 months to come up with the money. And by "money", I mean over half a million dollars… at the age of 23… with no credit and a laughable down payment. I spoke with loan agents, investors, and I even spoke with the owners of the building in desperate attempts to persuade them to lease it to me instead of selling it outright. I would certainly be able to pull off a lease agreement but buying it outright would have been more of a struggle. I was shot down time and time again. I remember sitting down with the loan officer, proposing to her what I was trying to do. It was a lovely, sunny afternoon. I had already drank my typical morning cup of ambition (Dunkin Donut's iced mocha coffee), had on my most professional outfit that I could scrounge out from underneath a pile of overused paint clothing in my room, and asked for quite a hefty loan. She did some math and laughed and sent me on my way. Instead of being discouraged and embarrassed, I thought *how unprofessional of her*.

At 23-years-old, I just didn't have the means to pull this off on my own. After the owners' generous time span had expired, we regretfully informed them that it just wasn't going to happen.

After a year and a half of trying to make this work, the building was now publicly up for sale (because of my dad and I) and we were unable to secure the financing. Talk about irony. It was heartbreaking. I had my eye on that prize for what seemed like a lifetime and I really, wholeheartedly believed that it would work out in my favor.

I kept going back to my gut feeling which was telling me that it wasn't meant to be. Like I've told you, I'm a firm believer that everything happens for a reason. If acquiring that building was meant to happen, then it would have. Simple as that.

I took a good long look at that "For Sale" sign, pulled myself together and moved on without looking back. It's important to let yourself "feel" for a minute. Or even for a couple days. Those feelings will hurt, but it's important not to ignore them. You need to know what it feels like to have something not work out to be able to really appreciate when things do. You can and will persevere through anything.

You will forever live in the past if you cannot learn to overcome quickly. There are some things in this world that you cannot change. There's no point in dwelling, overthinking, or moping around. Pack up your thoughts into a nice little storage compartment in your brain, put them away, and keep going. Keep truckin'. Better things will come, and down the road, you'll be thankful. Sometimes this may take a while. For me, it didn't hit until about a year later when I discovered that the old Ferebee's Motel had become available. All of a sudden, I realized why so many other potential locations hadn't panned out: I had had my eye on this place and dreamt about making it my own since I was a little girl.

The old Ferebee's Motel in Midlothian, Virginia. Built it the 1940s, it had been home to Champion Saddlery for the past 20 years. I had been eyeballing this building ever since I was a child. I always dreamed of how cool it would be to transform this old motel into a space for my boutique. I was still craving something with a story and some character, and the newer construction buildings just didn't have it.

I viewed this space many times. I mean literally, I would walk through Champion pretending to be a casual shopper, attending their big annual sales, etc. I memorized the layout and brainstormed over and over the possibilities for a few years before it ever became vacant. One night after work, I drove over to the space after Champion had closed down. It was one of the first times I had seen it after it had been completely emptied out. I walked the layout, alone. I studied every square inch of the building inside and out now that it wasn't full of boots and saddles. I started ripping up one corner of the carpet, not too much, just enough to see what the original flooring looked like. I couldn't really tell what all was going on under the carpet by just looking at that one tiny section. So, I stepped back, hands on my hips, sighed, and stared at this project wondering how much work it would be. I texted the landlord right then and there and told her I wanted to sign the lease. Before she could even reply, I began ripping up all the old carpet. In my head, it was already a done deal!

I hadn't announced it publicly yet. In fact, I hadn't even told anybody yet that I had made the decision. It happened so suddenly, I can't explain how I came to that decision other than it was just intuition that night when I was there alone, brainstorming. Normally I've got my friends, family, or vendors nearby, but something about being alone in an empty building had my gears turning. I posted this picture on our Facebook page, didn't add an explanation to it or anything, just simply captioned it "Renovations: Day 1" and then watched everybody's curiosity explode.

Perseverance takes time to build. It's not innate, we aren't born with it. It's something that is learned over time and through experience. Stay positive. People who have a constant negative attitude will never learn to overcome and continue blazing their trail. I've gotten myself to where I am today by trusting my instincts and making my own calculated decisions. Whether you've just started out, or you've got 10 years under your belt, you've done more than most people have! Even just getting started is a major accomplishment. Embrace it, trust yourself, trust the journey, and don't give up. As they say, good things come to those who wait – and *push* for it!

vision

*Learning how to use your creativity
to see the pretty in the ugly*

The ability to look at something horrific and see badass. To see the good underneath the bad. Am I the only one who gets upset watching all those home renovation shows on TV? The couple will immediately shoot down a property because it's not "move-in ready" and the whole time I'm just thinking about all the potential. Paint a couple walls, move a couple things around, and add some funky décor and BAM you have a whole new house.

When I think of "vision," the first specific moment that comes to mind is my beloved vintage 1960s Shasta compact camper, Penelope. I'm currently laughing at my laptop as I'm typing this because my camper is *that* bad. I mean, God bless her heart. I bought her the day before Christmas 2018. I had been working my butt off, and she was my Christmas gift to myself that year for a job well done. To Emily, from Emily. It was a particularly hard Christmas for me. It would be the very last holiday spent with both of my childhood dogs. I felt like this camper was a diamond in the rough, a blessing that was just dropped in my lap and acted as a kickstart for 2019.

I don't typically believe in luck, but this scenario was just too good to be true. This camper was in fairly decent shape compared to others that I had looked at and was listed at a fraction of the cost of most vintage campers that I had seen in the area.

Icing on the cake, it was located only about 45 minutes away from me. *No way*, I thought. These types of things just don't happen to me. But what could I lose by just reaching out to the man? So, I messaged him. Somehow, some way, it was still available. I was actually the first person to inquire about it, believe it or not.

I immediately drove out there, cash in hand. I walked around the camper for a couple minutes, inspecting it, even though I already knew I was going to buy it. I handed him the cash and a couple months later, had it towed to my store by one of my vendor's husband. He pulled it up to the front of the shop and I remember this moment clear as day. I quickly walked up to it, clapping my hands and just totally overcome with excitement. To finally have it in my possession, at my store, was a dream come true. It was quite possibly more exciting than the day I stepped off the school bus and saw my mom pulling up with my very first car—my precious blue 2000 Mercury Cougar (AKA the party bus).

As soon as I opened the camper door, a cockroach crawled out. Literally... a roach! The driver, wide-eyed, watched the cockroach scurry away and then he looked up at me and said, "You've got a lot of work on your hands."

I laughed in agreement.

This thing is literally no more than 20 square feet. And mind you, I had just spent 2 months of my life renovating a 3,500 square foot 75-year-old motel. This thing should be a piece of cake, right? A few new pieces of plywood, some paint, and lots of vision is all she needs! I sure wasn't going to let this little cockroach make me think any less of this beauty.

I ripped out that 1960s carpet which made the whole thing look like an cut-rate porn studio, took out the old lighting, and removed the wooden built-in seating. My neighbors like to take advantage of every chance they get to make fun of it. Luckily, I can look past the rust, the wasp nests, the ant infestation, the mold, and the old carpet. Sounds bad, doesn't it? But every time I look at her, I picture myself camping in the middle of nowhere, lying on my back on the bed with my legs crossed and a good book in hand.

She's much more than just a pile of junk sitting in my back parking lot. To me, she embodies everything that my life is about. Taking something that's debatably beyond repair and turning it into something amazing. When people question why there's an old trailer with a tarp covering it parked at my store, I like to remind them that she's got to get ugly before she gets pretty again! This has most definitely proven true during my days of renovations:

Day 1 of camper reno consisted of uncovering a whole section of massive flying ants underneath the floorboards. I let out a shriek as I began pulling back the carpet. I'd be willing to bet you could hear it all the way from the main road. I quickly jumped out of the camper and did what looked to be some sort of dance, desperately trying to shake off any ants that had found their way onto my body.

Nevertheless, I took a deep breath and stepped back into the camper, finished ripping out that carpet and disposed of it with a quickness.

OK, the worst part is over, right?

Wrong!

I began peeling back the water damaged ceiling panels. Being the smart cookie that I am, I stood right underneath the part that I was ripping off. To my own credit, there isn't very much room in there to stand to the side. Surely nothing gross could fall from a 1960s ceiling!

Naturally, an entire pile of molded insulation fell onto my head and got stuck in my hair. And the insulation would be home to none other than... drumroll please... another army of ants! Now, I know that I can be a little dramatic at times, but I really was convinced that this was undoubtedly the moment where I would die. It's OK, I've lived a great life and had a lot of fun, right? I could just see the headline now: "Girl Attacked in Old Camper by a Swarm of Killer Ants."

Needless to say, after this near-death experience, I took a couple days off from working on the camper. I may or may not have hired somebody to take out of the rest of the paneling for me. But shh, you didn't hear that from me, the DIY queen herself.

One day, they'll be no evidence of any remaining ant infestation or water damaged flooring. With a little vision, a little love, and a whole lot of hard work, Penelope will be good as new. She'll be thriving with a new look, a new purpose, and with me by her side!

I like to think of "vision" in multiple ways. I have to be able to see past a good amount of dirt and grime to see a diamond in the rough at an estate sale, but I also have to be able to see my goals in life and to visualize myself accomplishing them. I've always been told that if you visualize something hard enough, it will eventually come to fruition. See it happening to you, picture it, and with dedication it will happen. Think it into existence. Whenever I find myself struggling or feeling particularly unmotivated to do something, I try to visualize how I would feel if I was already there and had already accomplished it. That visualization helps to make it actually happen.

final thoughts

Let's wrap this thing up. I could honestly go
on and on, thinking of more traits that you might find
helpful, but the power to live a life of purpose and
passion ultimately lies within you. In navigating old
building renovations, run down camper projects,
tattered relationships, and career juggling, I've
undoubtedly learned that not everything is always

going to be perfect. In fact, nothing ever is because there is no such thing as perfection. We have to shift our focus away from chasing perfection and more towards just chasing what genuinely makes us happy. When there is happiness, failure as we know it ceases to exist.

You know, I've been working on this book for a couple years now and I've always wondered when a good time would be to put it out there for the world to see. Maybe there would be a better time to publish it, 5 or so years from now. Who knows what I would have accomplished by then and maybe I'd have even more to say and more experience under my belt.

But who am I kidding? There's always room to accomplish more and take yourself to new heights. You set little goals here and there, sure. You have your daily, weekly, monthly goals, but your lifetime goals change as you grow and evolve. There is never a point where you stop and think you are completely finished. And if you do get to that point, you're wrong. You. Are. Not. Done. You're just feeling comfortable and that's your brain's way of telling you that it's time to move on to the next big thing.

My point is "if not now, then when?" Writing has always been a dream of mine since I was a little girl. So here I am, writing. There is no better time than right here and right now to do *anything*. Stop waiting and start doing! You hear people every day talking about their dreams, desires, and things they want to accomplish but it's not as often that you see real action being taken. Action is the key, even if you have no idea what you're doing. Take the initiative, open that store, start that company, build your small business, be a better YOU! Reach for those daily goals and eventually each little goal that you achieve will add up to something amazing. Stop comparing yourself to others, being afraid to fail, making excuses for yourself, doubting your abilities. As they say, "go confidently in the direction of your dreams."

What motivates you? Stability or passion? There's nothing wrong with having a job that comes with great benefits and a steady paycheck (I wish my job came with those), but if it's not fulfilling your dreams and inner-most desires, then girl I'm here to tell you to kick it to the curb! There will always be somebody out there who will tell you never to quit your day job. Don't listen. If your passion is strong enough, you will always find a way to make it work and make ends meet.

Take these 14 traits and apply them to your everyday life. Integrate them into each and every thing you do. Commitment, self-worth, curiosity, intuition, self-discipline, integrity, morality, generosity, forgiveness, persistence, originality, innovation, perseverance, and vision. This is your toolbox full of all the necessities to be a great friend, wife, sister, mom, and *businesswoman*!

Be a yes person. Say YES to the things that set your soul on fire and say yes to the things that bring you an abundance of happiness and joy. But it's not enough just to say yes. You have to take that yes and carry it with you every day, holding it tight and staying true to it. Use that yes and turn it into a career, a path, and a life exploding with passion and limitless possibilities.

Made in USA - Kendallville, IN
1182116_9798621221348
10.19.2020 0819